Letters to Karen

Letters to Philip

Letters to Karen

Letters to Philip

On Keeping Love in Marriage

Charlie W. Shedd

VINE BOOKS
SERVANT PUBLICATIONS
ANN ARBOR, MICHIGAN

Vine Books is an imprint of Servant Publications especially designed to serve evangelical Christians.

Published by Servant Publications
P.O. Box 8617
Ann Arbor, Michigan 48107

Cover design: Left Coast Design, Portland, OR
Cover photograph: Westlight. Used by permission.

97 98 99 00 10 9 8 7 6 5 4 3 2 1

The publisher wishes to thank the publishers under whose imprints *Letters to Karen* and *Letters to Philip* first appeared: *Letters to Karen* was first published by Abingdon Press. © 1965 by Abingdon Press, Nashville, Tennessee, USA. All rights reserved. *Letters to Philip* was first published in 1968 by Bantam Doubleday Dell Publishing Group, Inc. © 1968 by Charlie W. Shedd and the Abundance Foundation. Published by arrangement with Doubleday, a division of Bantam Doubleday Dell Publishing Group, Inc.

Printed in the United States of America
ISBN 1-56955-029-8

LIBRARY OF CONGRESS CATALOGING-IN-PUBLICATION DATA

Shedd, Charlie W.
Letters to Karen; and, Letters to Philip : on keeping love in marriage / Charlie W. Shedd.
p. cm.
First work originally published: Letters to Karen. Nashville, Tenn. : Abingdon Press, 1965. 2nd work originally published: Letters to Philip. New York : Bantam Doubleday Dell, 1968.
ISBN 1-56955-029-8
1. Marriage. 2. Love. 3. Interpersonal relations. 4. Shedd, Charlie W.—Correspondence. 5. Shedd, Karen—Correspondence. 6. Shedd, Philip—Correspondence. 7. Fathers—Correspondence. I. Shedd, Charlie W.—Letters to Philip. II. Title. III. Title: Letters to Philip.
HQ734.S535 1997
306.81—dc21 97-23714
CIP

Foreword

What are the three most important words in any marriage?

"I love you"?

"You are beautiful"?

"Please forgive me"?

Yes, all these words are very important. But are they the most important? No. The three most important words in any marriage are ... "TALK, TALK, TALK!"

Why? Because without "talk, talk, talk," the "I love you" will not get through. Neither will "you are beautiful" or "please forgive me."

Thirty years have passed since *Letters to Karen* and *Letters to Philip* were written. And in those thirty years Martha and I received thousands of letters from readers. Beautiful letters. Letters sharing their ideas. Letters crying for help. Letters singing their joy. But none more meaningful than this from a grateful wife in Brazil:

> *Dear Dr. Shedd:*
>
> *My husband, he no talk. He good man, but he very busy. He provide well for me and our children. But he hardly ever talk.*
>
> *So we go to our priest and tell him we are unhappy. You know what he do? He give us your* Letters to Karen *and* Letters to Philip. *He tell us, "Read these. They will help you." We do that, and they did.*
>
> *So now we talk every day and it is beautiful.*
>
> *Thank you,*
> *Juanita*

My publishers tell me there is no way to know how many people have read *Letters to Karen* and *Letters to Philip*. Translated into more than twenty languages; used in the offices of doctors, counselors, ministers; studied as textbooks in high schools, colleges, and churches. The number of copies in circulation will be forever unknown. So?

So, one of my publishers said, "Why should we worry about numbers? Let's call it the 'multi-million bestseller' and praise the Lord."

Yes, praise the Lord and thank you, all you readers. Plus from the heart of this author, thank you Servant Publications. Through this, your wedding gift edition, many more will say:

"So now we talk every day and it is beautiful."

So thank you, readers.
Thank you, publishers.
Thank you, Lord.

From the grateful author,
Charlie Shedd

Letters to Karen

On Keeping Love in Marriage

Contents

Marriage…

is not so much *finding* the right person as it is *being* the right person!

Preface

This is for Karen. She is one of the fair young daughters of Eve who grace our land. Karen is many things. She is chiefly a lover of peace. But for combat she is armed with cunning. (She has four brothers.) In jeans and sweat shirt she has all the charm of the girl next door. Then again, dressed for the ball, she bears herself with elegance. At times she is somewhat of a romp. Yet on other occasions she would go with you to the deepest interiors.

Ardent and adorable, comely and clever, winsome and wise—that's Karen!

I'm her dad. I know what you're thinking, and you are right. There are *some* prejudiced fathers. But if you know Karen as I know Karen, you would say, "Now speakest thou the truth plainly!"

Several months before she was married, Karen asked me to write her some special letters. "Daddy," she said at her beaming best, "I'd like you to tell me how I can keep him loving me forever!"

There are two reasons why my daughter would make such a request. For one thing, I am a pastor. As such, I have discussed matrimonial matters with countless couples. I have also spent many hours with wives alone and husbands by themselves.

This is nothing unusual these days. Most of my clergyman friends are caught up in the marriage entanglements of their people.

What can we do?

Sometimes very little. This is especially true when their minds are already set. They come for agreement, not advice. Occasionally one wants to negotiate, but the other will not.

So we can only watch in horror while another home crashes on the hard rocks of charges, counter-charges, bitterness, and revenge.

As you would do, we try to lend a hand in picking up the pieces. This is especially difficult if there are children. They may remind us of broken eggs whose nests have been blown from beneath them.

Then we have our good days when everything goes well. Frequently, this is not our doing. We sense a mysterious visitation, some "holy hunch," which could only come from wisdom greater than our own.

Now we may witness one of the pastor's big thrills. The quarrelers kiss and make up. "Chords which were broken will vibrate once more."

That's how it is. Bewilderment to keep us wondering! Failure to keep us humble! Success to keep us trying! So, anymore, as they come through my study door I join the Brittany fishermen in their winsome prayer, "Keep us, O God! The sea is so big and our boats are so little!"

You will agree it was a reasonable request which my daughter made. Certain rules apply to every marriage. Yet each wedding also creates a pattern which will develop its own unique involvements.

Accordingly, these letters left my mailbox with a father's prayer that they might be useful to one woman and her beloved.

But most of us need every possible aid for better fulfilling the laws of love. We need help in learning the language of devotion.

Because this is true, these letters are offered here with the added wish that they may be helpful to others—young, mature, older—as they accept this challenge.

Is there any greater hope than this? If we *can* succeed in building happier homes, we have the satisfaction of knowing that we have helpED this much to create a healthy society.

I said there are two reasons why my particular daughter might ask me to write some answers to her question. As I was saying, she is an astute young lady. She knows how little her dad really knows. But she also knows another thing.

Reason two is the subject of letter one.

Charlie W. Shedd

"Exhibit A"

My dear Karen,

You always were a clever little thing, and I see you have lost none of your touch.

They say, "Flattery will get you everywhere!" It did this time. You sent me quickly to my typewriter. Wouldn't any father swell with pride before such admiration? Imagine that! *My* daughter thinks that much of *my* opinions.

But when I sat down to begin, a great light dawned!

Your request *is* a superb compliment, but it is not for me. For twenty years you have been observing "Exhibit A!"

Therefore, brought low once more by your trickery, I accept your proposal as the magnificent bouquet to your mother which it really is.

You know how devoid I am of knowledge in many areas. But you also know that on one item I *am* an unmitigated authority. Firsthand, I understand how good it is to be loved by a genius in the art of being a wife.

It will be fun describing my favorite person, so I'll be writing you again real soon.

Love, Dad

We Know in Part

My dear Karen,

When you were in high school you went with many boys. We watched on tiptoe when some new date came to the house. Would this be *the* one?

If my memory serves me correctly, not one of them was a total collapse. We admired your taste. They were all nice-looking. Even the big clown who was "so homely he's cute," as you put it, wasn't overly hard on our eyes.

We liked something about every boy you ever dated.

(Come to think of it, there was that one you said reminded you of "a stray puppy looking for a home." We thought he'd never go away. He was the nearest to an exception.)

We would discuss them between us, your mother and I, and we were proud of your friends. They were well-mannered, clean-cut, nicely groomed when they should be, and "such good drivers." This last is what you told us, and I guess you are living proof of your claim.

That giant he-man football player took our eye. He must have spent a fortune calling you long-distance. He reminded us of a Saint Bernard dog—huge, but so gentle and leisurely.

Then came a night I'll never forget. It was after you had dated him for some time. I was still up when you came in, and you announced that you had just crossed him off your list, too. You know how it is with fathers. I was afraid that something unpleasant had happened.

"No," you assured me, "he's so sweet. But, Daddy, could we visit a little right now?"

As nearly as I can recall them your exact words were: "I worry sometimes about me. It seems as if all the boys I ever go with are just darling for a while and then I get bored. After a few dates it's as if I knew all there is to know. Do you think there's something wrong with me? I'm scared when I think about getting married. How could I possibly spend my whole life with one man? Do you suppose I'll ever find one interesting enough to keep my attention forever?"

Of course I assured you that someday one would appear, riding from out of somewhere, and he would have ample soul to keep you entertained for always. You said you weren't sure I was right. Then you made this speech which rang the deep bells in my heart.

You took me by the hand and said, "Daddy, I made a big decision tonight. I'm never, ever going to get married unless I meet a boy who is so great it will take a whole lifetime to know everything there is about him."

I thought this was terrific. That night you reached out and touched the pulse of your future husband.

Time passed and suddenly your question marks stood erect like exclamation points!!!

The first we knew of this was one evening about supper time. You called from the university, do you remember? There was a delightful new awe in your voice. You said, "Daddy, there is this perfectly fabulous boy who waits tables in our dorm. He's the most interesting person I've ever met. He's been around the world so many times." (That's what you said, but I guess it's only twice, isn't it? Can a fellow make it more often than that in the Navy unless he's a career man?)

Like a lovely brook you babbled on, "He knows so much more than I do about everything. And is he ever smart! He understands all about television. That's his major. And he's practically an authority on Latin America. That's his other major. Oh, yes, I forgot to tell you his name is Vincent! Isn't that the most beautiful name? He's worked his way through school and done more things. Besides, he's handsome, and you never saw anybody who understands people like he does. Everybody just loves him because he can talk about any subject they bring up.

"And, Daddy, you know how crazy you and Mother were about Greece? Well, he knows everything about Greece. His ship was stationed there for three weeks."

And so on, and so on, and so on.

I recall clearly that you had me so much in orbit with you I even temporarily forgot this was a collect call. It flashed through my mind that I'd have to ask my friend Jim (he's division manager of the telephone company) if there might be special rates for historical occasions.

Then you threw another bunch of stars at me and away we went once more. Finally, I came back to earth again, and it occurred to me that people in the parish do have emergencies and we'd better open the phone lines at some future date, just in case.

Finally, we agreed that as soon as he could get time off from his many jobs he should drive you home in his dreamy little Volkswagen and let the whole family see for themselves.

"What was *that* all about?" one of your brothers asked when I hung up. "That," I announced, "was about Karen's future husband!" "Her *what?*" they shouted in unison, and we really had ourselves a family pow-wow that night.

Then you brought him home, and we saw what you meant. Here was the dream man your heart was calling to that evening as we sat discussing those tremendous things together.

One of the greatest things ever written on love is 1 Corinthians 13. The next time you read it, notice that the only repetition in the entire chapter is this:

"*We know in part!*"

The writer seems to be saying, "Back up and have one more look at the endless vistas of love. Here is something you must consider again. Beauty in human relations does not require total knowledge all at once."

We can be everlastingly thankful for this in many ways. For one thing, am I ever glad people can't see all the way through me! Then, when we go back and review it again, isn't it also fine that we don't know all about other people? If it weren't for this double protection we'd probably all join in that crazy chorus, "Stop the world, I want to get off!"

But when it applies to marriage, this is nothing less than a stupendous gift. To be married to someone in whom you see islands to be discovered, mountains to climb, valleys to explore, and new wonders beckoning off in the distance—this *is* absolutely the greatest.

It does create some problems though. You can't learn how to handle people such as this all at once. It's true the days will never grow dull if you once begin this journey. Yet, on the other hand, it may also be exasperating sometimes.

So when you feel like saying, "Men! Why *does* my husband do such crazy things? Will I every understand what makes him act like that?"—when you feel this way, you just be grateful for a man you *can't* comprehend all at once.

This beauty of a partial knowledge is what makes life with your loved ones so fascinating. It could exhaust you if you let it. But it can also keep your heart singing with the thrill of just being alive.

Your mother and I have been married twenty-six years, and—this is the truth—new thrills come fresh from her soul every day. I'm still finding out things about her I never knew before—still thankful for someone so tremendous it will take me a lifetime to search her out fully—still glad of heart the whole day long that "we know in part."

You will remember Aletha. She helped us take care of you when you were little. She worked part-time, but she left a full-time imprint. We came to be the kind of friends where you don't worry what you say around each other. That is why, when we became a bit parent-cross or if we spoke too harshly to one of you, she would gather you up in her arms and say, "Aw, now! All they needs is a great big bunch of waitin' on the Lord!"

That's a great word for parenthood. It also works magic for a man and woman seeking to blend two lives together.

Don't push too hard! Pray for patience! Give each other room to grow!

Listen! Do you hear what I hear? It's a distant sound and deep, like a drummer drumming. I hope you like it. We'll hear him often at his theme as we go along together, and these are the words which fit the beat:

Marriage is not a ceremony! This is a creation!

Yours for joy in the vast unknown,
Dad

Happiness Is to Grow Up

My dear Karen,

Many couples make the mistake of thinking that two saying "I do!" means "We did it!" They assume that by the mere act of climbing the chancel steps they have already vaulted the stairs into seventh heaven.

Some sociologists say this originates with the Hollywood moon-glow in our movies and television. Others blame the romantic writers. Or is it the fault of the songmakers?

Right now, tracing the source is not important as a full understanding of this fact:

Marriage may be "made in heaven" in the original. But the whole deal is more like one of those kits which comes knocked down for putting together. It will take some gluing here, sanding rough spots there, hammering a bit now, filing down the scratches on this side, planing a bit on that side, carving a piece, bending this section slightly, varnishing, backing off for a frequent look, dusting, waxing, polishing, until at last what you have is a thing of beauty and a joy forever.

If you will look in the "H" section of your American College Dictionary, you will find these important words: "*Happiness results from ... attainment of what one considers good.... Contentment is a peaceful kind of happiness in which one rests without desires, even though every wish may have been gratified."*

These words apply to even the best unions. Marriage does not suddenly make imperfect people perfect. Every human being has some flaws. This sweeping statement, I regret to inform you, *does* include Vincent. It also includes you.

Handling such a challenge is largely a matter of mature thinking. Every one of us at some earlier date has been in love with the "dream image" of what our perfect lover would one day be. If either of you insists on clinging to your fantasy unduly, you may be in so for some real disappointments.

I recall one young bride who returned from her honeymoon quite upset. She had married a much older man. We all thought it might be a good match under their particular set of circumstances. But she came to me considerably shaken. She said she simply hadn't been able to recover from the first night when he took out his teeth and put them in a glass on the hotel dresser. He insisted on a soft light during their lovemaking. But those infernal choppers leering at her from the glass cut her response to nil. She knew he had false teeth. But she had never inquired what he did with them at night!

Thank goodness, most of the cruel blows which shatter our "ideal mate" are not quite that garish. But they will come. So it is important that you "put away childish things." One such is whatever may be left of the phantom heroes of your girlhood.

If you hang on too tightly you may risk a couple of serious errors. You could waste a good deal of time and energy trying to make your man over into something he was never meant to be. You might also be concentrating so much on *what he is not* that you become blind to some of the fine things which make him what he is.

With almost everyone whom we learn to know well, we discover that certain defects are part of the price they pay for their virtues. An attractive person is not so much a collection of miscellaneous parts, good and bad, strewn about. What makes him appealing is more likely to be the way in which he has organized those parts.

The same thing goes for homemaking. In a vital marital combination two wise persons are trying to organize their parts in oneness which will be good for both of them. To see each other work on this, to help each other accomplish this, is one of the dynamics of marriage at its best.

So don't let glamour victimize you. You are not flawless yourself, and you'd be very uncomfortable if Vincent should prove the first exception to this rule—boys have blemishes and young men come unfinished to the wedding.

Take an honest look at his faults. Look in the mirror at your own weaknesses. Then study how you can fit your two sets of faults into your two sets of strong point to make the best blending possible.

When you marry, you become more vulnerable to disappointment and hurt than you have ever been before. But you have decided it is worth the risk.

You have chosen wisely. Only by taking this chance can you become eligible for the bliss which is two people "oneing" themselves together.

There is an anonymous essay in my files which is a favorite of ours. It is written by a ten-year-old boy named Tommy for his school composition. There are two words here which stand out in bold relief against the background of future happiness. This is his theme:

What Is Love?

Love is something that makes two people think they are pretty even when nobody else does. It also makes them sit close together on a bench even when there's plenty of room. It's something which makes two people very quiet when you are around. And when they think you're gone they talk about roses and dreams. And that's all I know about love until I grow up!

Let's hope he's one of the fortunate who learns that love grows finer if you find someone with whom you can share these two key words:

"Grow up!"

Good for Tommy! Good also for Karen and Vincent and every one of us faced with the challenge of bringing roses and dreams to reality behind our own doors.

We like to believe that you are both mature for your age. We never forget that maturity is in part knowing where you need to become more mature.

We have heard you say, "Vincent and I are terribly in love." Whether your love is terribly terrific or terribly terrible may depend sometimes on Tommy's two words: "*Grow up!*"

Best wishes for a maturing love,
Dad

Let Freedom Ring

My dear Karen,

"Divine Wedlock" is an ecclesiastical term which has a nice solid ring wherever you hear it. In two words it seems to bring together that hallowed security which just about everybody hopes to find someday.

But you do well to understand that this is never right unless there are two keys to the lock. You are each entitled to one of these, and they are yours to use in wisdom.

"Everything I Have Is Yours!" "You Can Have Me if You Want Me, but You Must Be Mine Alone!" "Why Not Take All of Me?"—this sort of thing may go well in the slushy songs of the sentimentalists. But marriage at its best does not live by the code of the jukebox. It lives by the gradual integration of two people who give each other plenty of room for personal development.

Like so many other things in husband-wife relationships, there is a fine line here. Because each marriage represents the bringing together of two unique persons, no one can tell exactly where the "liberty line" is best marked off in your union. It will take careful testing and stretching to find yours together.

Right now I am working with a young wife who was on the receiving end of a big shock recently. Her husband announced that he wanted one night out each week, and, in addition, he did not expect to report where he had been. He simply put his request calmly and told her he would give her some time to think it over.

This was particularly hard for Sally. They had been married less than six months, and she grew up with the idea that "when you marry you tell each other everything."

But this is an astute young lady. She agreed to think it over and sought help for the right answer. As we discussed it, she began looking for clues in his background.

Here is an excellent starting place when someone has hurt you. You know that others often do odd things *to* you for reasons which did not originate *with* you. They may be "working through" a childhood repression, "surfacing" some old conflict, or struggling again with a problem which began long before you knew each other.

A wholesome sympathy based on understanding often has a clarifying effect on both of you. If you can keep the tears out of your eyes long enough, you may be able to "see" where he is blind. And if you learn to project your "love-light" carefully, you may contribute to his own "self-transparency," So, whenever you are wounded, try to begin at the point of saying, "Perhaps this is *his* problem. Before I let it become mine, let's see if it can be an occasion for our maturing together."

This is true bigness, isn't it? It requires a high level of maturity to "act" in love rather than to "react" with hostility.

Thank goodness Sally was big enough to take her mind off her own wounds and focus on his. She knew that Jeff was the youngest of several children. There had never been the privacy in his home which she was allowed in hers. He was not permitted the precious little secrets of childhood. His parents were making decisions for him long after he should have been making them for himself. In his teens he was subjected to an inquisition following every date. She also knew that his father was basically distrustful of everyone, including members of his own family.

As she talked about the problem, she considered several possibilities. She toyed with the idea of retaliation. She might ask for one night out in seven on *her* own with no accounting. But she decided this was not her best move.

"At first," she said, "this might keep him home but it wouldn't solve the problem. He needs to think that someone has complete faith in him. Besides," she admitted, "a night out by myself would be a bore to me!"

Then she made a statement which I wrote down after she left. You might like to memorize this:

"I decided," she concluded, "that maybe *it would be smart if I let him think I am all his and he is all his own!*"

That is a remarkable observation for one in the tender first year of marriage, don't you think?

So, she granted him his request. One exciting night out each week with no reporting to anyone.

This has been going on for three months now and guess what's happening! Jeff is spending more and more of those "free nights" at home or taking her out. Her secret formula is doing its job so well that he even volunteered last week to tell her where he had been going. Every one of those evenings by himself he had either been to a movie alone or shooting billiards with the boys. That's what he said, and I believe him.

You can see that Sally, by her feminine prudence, has led him to the sense of freedom which he needs. But, unknown to himself, she is actually drawing him closer to herself. You sense, of course, that the next step up in their marriage will come when he catches on and begins to be equally wise in handling her.

I see some men who never get the message. They operate under the delusion that a successful husband is one who imprisons "the little woman" within the prison of *his* desires.

Some women give in to this treatment and resign their individuality. But this is not living, and it is never marriage at its best. "Togetherness" isn't always healthy. It may be what my psychiatrist friends call "symbiotic." In everyday language this means that two different kinds of emotional illness have come together in a manner which supports them both for a period, or perhaps for a lifetime.

This is not for folks such as you. No wife is in her right place if she is crushed under the total domination of a tyrant husband. You will recognize at once that the same thing applies vice versa.

So, I hope you'll both remember this interesting paradox about "togetherness." It must include whatever amount of "apartness" is right for each of you. And if you allow plenty of room for the "apartness," this has a way of magnetizing the "togetherness."

In other words, the more you can be free *from* each other without resentment when you feel the need for freedom, the more you will be free *with* each other in sharing your full selves.

Some of the best psychologists I know tell me that mental health depends in large measure on a person's ability to discover his real self and disclose it to at least one other person. Wise couples accept this and begin building these two-way streets early in their marriage.

In our last letter we talked about "growing up." In another we'll discuss "growing outward." We will also consider "going out together." Here let's note that some "going out alone" may be good stuff for the first layers of that healthy escape route which may circle around to bring you closer to each other in the end.

Down this road you should permit each other to go some places where you keep up special interests which appeal to you alone. You can have friends which are your very own, and he can have some which are his. Certain matters which seem like trivia to you may be very important to him. The same is true from your side. (Of course, all this can be overdone, and some couples overdo it.) But mature mates will leave off their cooing long enough to provide whatever freedom is essential for developing their individuality as they develop their oneness.

This mutual independence is actually a large part of your heritage. Your background in home, church, school, and nation has provided you with the cardinal concepts of this great way of life.

Therefore, seek to make your dwelling place a little republic, inhabited first by two citizens, later by others, each with sacred rights and privileges of his own. Don't over-invade each other's privacy. Don't hold on so tight that you squeeze one another away.

This is a big order for a woman who loves her man so much that she wants to share everything with him all at once. You love Vincent that much. You want to be "all his" and long for him to be "all yours." We know he feels the same toward you.

But I've got news for you—you will only reach the sublime heights of perfect union if you pledge each other freedom enough to develop the original creation which is the "high, holy place" in each individual.

This is Divine Wedlock—two people growing both individually and in unity until they become what they were meant to be together.

Let freedom ring,

Dad

Yours For Fun

My dear Karen,

Thought you might enjoy something from your own family background.

In musing on the imperfections which turn up in our "perfect" sweethearts after the wedding I remembered this one.

When we were first married your mother couldn't abide my habit of leaving the dresser drawers open. But I honestly thought this is how it was supposed to be. A man wants a shirt? So he makes his selections from the top drawer and leaves the drawer open. He needs socks? Make the choice from drawer three and leave it open.

I'm telling you the truth—I thought that closing drawers was one reason God created women. My mother had been closing dresser drawers behind me for twenty-two years.

But in less than twenty-two hours I discovered that my new bride simply couldn't tolerate this utter thoughtlessness.

I am almost embarrassed to tell you what sent me into tantrums in her behavior. I discovered to my horror that this beautiful creature I was tied to forever had a horrendous habit—*she squeezed the toothpaste tube in the middle rather than carefully rolling it from the bottom!* (You see right here that there are some things you might not find out about your "intended" before marriage.)

Why did she do this awful thing? Because she had always squeezed it that way. Her family couldn't care less about toothpaste tubes.

But they did care about drawers. For them, closing drawers was a symbol of things done decently and in order. It also had another meaning. It signified that each member of the household was being considerate of every other member.

Of course, it all seems silly now. This, incidentally, is another of the nice things life has a way of doing for us. It makes things look funny from a distance which were anything but that close up.

I hope you'll have a million laughs as you open up the clown-rooms inside yourselves.

Yours for fun,
Dad

Emphasis On the Good Things

My dear Karen,

High on the list of happy marriages which your mother and I have known is the union between Bob and Helen J.

On the surface they seem to have little in common. Bob is a pusher and she is retiring. He is the life of the party. You'll usually find her in the shadows. But they are radiantly in love.

We noticed it first at a banquet while some visiting speaker was giving his address. Part of the time they held hands. Now and then they looked at each other with a sly smile, as if they were reading loud and clear some silent message between them.

Then one night we were invited to dinner at their house. You would have loved it. He went to the kitchen a couple of times, and I heard him ask if there was anything he could do. Once she said, "No thanks, honey. Take it easy!" The next time she let him pour the water.

When we went to the table he held her chair and then, of all things, he *served her first!* I don't know what the etiquette books say about this, but my guess is it wouldn't have shamed him one bit. And she didn't protest. She sat there glowing as if this were the way to do things and wasn't life wonderful?

It was.

The whole dinner was a thing of beauty. Several times in the conversation he asked her opinion on some subject and even listened while she told what she thought about it. When the meal was finished, he rose to help her clear the table.

After dinner, while he and I were alone in the den, I decided to find out more about this. "Bob," I said, "you and Helen seem so perfectly adjusted to each other. I've watched you for some time now, and I think it's great. I see so many unhappy marriages. Do you have any secrets I might pass on to others?'

He laughed a bit more in hesitation than embarrassment. In a few moments he recited a story which I think is a classic.

"We had a terrible time when we were first married," he began. "In fact, we even talked about calling it quits. Then we read something that gave us an idea. We decided to make a list of all the things we didn't like about each other. Of course, it was hard, but Helen gave me hers and I gave her mine. It was pretty rough reading. Some of the things we had never said out loud or shared in any way.

"Next, we did something which might seem foolish so I hope you won't laugh. We went to the trash basket in the backyard and burned those two lists of bad things. We watch them go up in smoke and put our arms around each other for the first time in a long while.

"Then we went back into the house and made a list of all the good things we could dig up about each other. This took some time, since we were pretty down on our marriage. But we kept at it and when we finished we did another thing which might look silly. Come on back to the bedroom and I'll show you."

It was a neat room, lots of light, and a happy spread on the big old bed from grandma's house.

But at the focal point in that bedroom wall there were two plain maple frames, and in them what do you suppose?

In one was the list of the good things Helen could see in Bob. In the other was his scribbled list of her virtues. That's all there was. Just two scratchy lists behind glass.

"If we have any secret," Bob continued, "I guess this is it. We agreed to read these things at least once a day. Of course, we know them by heart now. I couldn't begin to tell you what they've done for me. I recite them to myself sometimes when I'm driving the car or waiting for a customer. When I hear fellows complain about their wives I think of my list and thank my lucky stars. Funny, too, the more I consider the good she sees in me the more I try to be like that. And when I really understand her good points I tried all the harder to build on these. Now I think she's the most wonderful person in the world. I guess she sort of likes me too. That's all there is to it!"

That's *all*, the man says!

But it goes right to the heart of great marriage. This kind of love has a way of gradually canceling out the bad and raising up the good.

You'll be interested to know that I have suggested Bob and Helen's technique many times in marriage counseling. I've seen it work real miracles. Sometimes they had simply forgotten the great thoughts they held for each other before the ring exchange. Usually these things slip away on padded feet. Before we know it the affirmative has disappeared and our thoughts are slanted in the direction of "She's all right *but*" or "He'd be so much nicer *if only!*"

Of course, you must face up to the negatives, and we'll get to this later. But you will be more attractive to each other in the home, you will learn to appreciate the good in others outside your walls, and they will more readily recognize the best in you if you slant your marriage in this direction.

Here is another word from 1 Corinthians 13 which is worth weaving into the fabric of your thoughts: *"Love does not rejoice at wrong but rejoices in the right."*

Positively,
Dad

Tell Him He's Wonderful

My dear Karen,

Have I ever told you about the little girl's essay on "What Makes a Marriage Great?" She wrote, "I guess it's when you love each other the right way, or enough, or something. I think to make a marriage great you have to treat each other like company a lot of the time and be polite and stuff like that!"

While couples are courting, they usually give considerable thought to ways and means of pleasing each other. "What can I do to make him happy?" and "I wonder if she would like this?" are common questions on the wooer's list.

It is a wise couple who continue this expression of their love into marriage and even increase it as the years pass. I'm not contending for words alone. Sometimes by your actions you can "speak" the depths of your feeling. A silent bit of tenderness well done at the right time may get your message through every bit as much as if you have said it out loud.

But a whole host of husbands and wives never approach the maximum. Three sad words describe many a marriage—"They quit courting." Sometimes this happens all at once. More likely it leaves the place gradually as they begin to take each other for granted.

Let me tell you about an experiment which I conducted recently. (I hate to do this because it shows us men up as the clods we really are, but let's face it!) One Sunday morning I left the pulpit early, turned the closing moments over to our associate pastor, and slipped up to the custodian's second-floor closet. His window overlooks the parking lot, and I wanted to watch the congregation leaving for home.

What I was about was to count the gentlemen-husbands who still open the car door for their wives.

It is safe to assume that ten out of ten did this little extra during their pre-marriage dating. But behold how the vision splendid fades!

The sad statistics are these: Only *three husbands in every ten* made their way to the opposite side of their automobiles to assist their ladies aboard. For seven out of ten it was as though by marrying these strong noblemen they had gained enough strength to open the car door for themselves!

These are all nice people, you understand, but they have fallen into that common error of those three sad words: "They quit courting!"

Important question here: *Will your marriage see an increase or a decrease in the little chivalries which make all the difference between a continuing romance and just another marriage?* Your answer may depend on the little girl's all-important directive—"be polite and stuff like that!"

Yet this emphasis on "doing" is not meant to minimize the importance of well-chosen words sincerely spoken at strategic times. This is one of the least expensive ingredients in the great marriages I have known. But it too does a steady fadeaway unless you consciously cultivate it daily.

If you were to knock on every door in any block and ask how

long it has been since hubby complimented wife, or vice versa, you might be surprised. The truth is that many married couples seem to have a filter on their lips preventing the passage of a kind word. Yet here is something which costs nothing, makes life more bearable, and sets the heart singing.

One night at a men's meeting, with you in mind, I asked those in attendance to write a few words on the subject, "What My Wife's Compliments Mean to Me."

Here are a few excerpts selected from more than forty statements:

> "Compliments? You bet! Like this writer guy I read puts it, 'I bring home the bacon and she furnishes the applesauce.'"

> "I think complimenting each other is one of the most important things in marriage. Whenever she praises me I feel as if she is pouring a larger mold. I have to grow bigger to fill it."

> "My wife is my most ardent fan and my best press agent."

Nice, aren't they? May it ever be so with you. But perhaps to give the full picture. I should add some which must have come from barren hearts. (I asked them not to sign their names.)

> "I run a store and my wife reminds me of those women who come stomping down the aisles looking for the manager."

> "My wife never compliments me. I feel sometimes like saying, 'Oh, for gosh sakes, quit your harping and go get a horn.'"

> "There is one man in our club whose wife is always praising her husband. I wish I had a woman like that. My wife doesn't know any compliments. She's on a constant safari looking for my faults."

"These are they which come out of great tribulation" and may it never be so for Vincent. Remember, my darling daughter, you can keep him loving you forever if you learn a thousand different ways to tell him he's wonderful.

But you better learn how to do this right. There are some important points to keep in mind.

For one thing, if you come at it nicely, *appreciation can be the background for showing him his faults.* Every couple in marriage should be growing toward personal betterment on both sides, or their union is stuck on dead center. We'll be seeing more of this when we discuss the art of disagreement and telling the truth in love. But right here it's enough to remember that varnish always melts under heat. You can only tell him isn't wonderful where he isn't if you have told him he is wonderful where he is.

You will also be wise to *watch for signs that you aren't giving him adequate nourishment for his ego.* Most husbands now and then overpraise themselves. When yours does this too much, it may mean that he needs more of your praise. Watch for it also when you are with others. If he pushes the crowd away from the footlights and demands top billing for himself, this may be your fault. Come out of the balcony and move to the front row.

Another indicator is oversensitivity. Whenever he is ultradefensive of his own prestige, when his happiness depends entirely on the nod of a head outside your walls, you're not slipping—you've slipped.

Comes now another cue for the clever wife. *Every man has certain areas where he's particularly pleased if his woman applauds.* This can be a secret little game you play between you. If you play it well, he may grow beyond it until he doesn't need it any more. But it will be important at the outset because most every man is not as good as he would like to be at some points. Your mother was an ace at this in our early days together. As you know, I played football, baseball, basketball, and nearly every game with a ball in it. Because I was big, I got by rather well at some of these. But the truth is that I was lazy.

As I look back over the gridirons and diamonds and courts where I played, I was never as good as I would like to have been. But there *was* one spot where I was a walloping success. (Well, anyway, for a time I was!) This was in wrestling. As you know, I still hold a title back in my home state. So, what if it is the record for being thrown quicker than anyone else in the heavyweight finals? I loved wrestling, and I was right there in the thick of it. Then I met my match, and Goliath went down with a resounding thud.

Yet, you'd never have known all this from your mother. She guarded my secret until I was grown up enough to tell it myself. She skillfully cast my praises about. Then, as your husband will, her husband made it over the hump. He decided to come clean. Yours, too, will have these places of pride and places of shame. You will do well to learn them and play to the gallery. It may take time, but, as the years are sure to pass anyway, you can both have fun with this diversion. Wise wives are like that.

But having rid ourselves of this bit of chicanery, let's transfer the thought to the thing which counts most. When love is done playing, when it reaches its best, *sincerity is an absolute must for the phrases of praise.*

Some atomizerlike women go giddily spraying their vapors all over the place. Yet, though men may appear to enjoy it, most males want more than chattery flattery from the women they love. (I like this apt phrase making the rounds of our high school gang these days: "Take the roof off the greenhouse, mother! The corn is getting taller!") So be sure your words have the feel of the real. He needs the authentic from you.

The postman is due. But before I seal the envelope, let's roll them over our tongues once more: "I think you're wonderful!"

If ever one sentence weighed a ton this is it. I hope Vincent will join your hallelujah chorus. May he sing it often in varied ways. But even if he doesn't, stop longing and begin it yourself. If he is as normal as I think he is, there will be a reaction and it will be good.

Whenever you see a radiant woman, you can be sure she knows she is loved. The same thing goes for men of genuine confidence.

You can bring out the best in each other if you look for the best and put it in words.

With all good wishes for all good praises,
Dad

P.S. There is an old story which supposedly comes from Vermont. They say this old grouch lived with his wife for twenty-one years and never spoke one single word. Then one morning at breakfast he broke the silence with, "Darling, sometimes when I think how much you mean to me it is almost more than I can do to keep from telling you!" (We'll hope it's only a New England folk tale.)

Moods! Moods! Moods!

My dear Karen,

Last night before you left for school you asked me, "Can't I do something about these awful moods?" You said Vincent was "down in the dumps," and I could see you were aching inside.

Let's begin with a fact which you must face: *Moods are a natur-*

al part of every personality. In my experience there are no exceptions among men. (Nor women or children either for that matter.) The only variation to the rule is one of degree or place or time or what motivates the mood. "Sometimes I'm up, sometimes I'm down" is the song of every soul. Even the saints flagged in zeal part of the time.

Come to think of it, isn't this escalator-going-both-ways a part of all life? Music has its somber fugues and gay roundelays. Nature has its cycles. History has its high times and low. It appears that all things fluctuate and husbands are no exception.

Be grateful for the blessings of contrast which these experiences provide. When our loved ones have bad moods, this may make their good stand out in bold relief after the agony has run its course. Perhaps we can appreciate our mates at their best because we are allowed to see them also at their worst.

Maybe you are asking, "But don't moods sometimes move from natural to 'sick'?" They certainly do, and one measurement is the time it takes for emerging. Any moody mind which returns rapidly to the sunshine indicates a healthy climate inside. It is good also to check for frequency. Are the morose moments coming with increasing rapidity? Another evil omen is the roller-coaster pattern—way up one day, way down the next! When these intensify at an alarming rate, you best hurry on down for advice from those who deal daily in troubled minds.

Comes now another item of real importance. *Try your best not to go down into the swamps of despair when he goes down.* This is much easier said than done, of course, and it will take some time to learn this one. It is so easy for you to become melancholy when he becomes melancholy.

Because you love him so much you want to share all things with him fully, and it may appear on the surface that you could help him best by glumming it through together! But "togetherness" of the highest kind does not mean going together to the lowest levels.

If you can keep your heart filled with high-level kindness when he is down, you will really contribute more to his recovery than by almost any other method. This may make him furious at first because most of us have never completely conquered this one subconscious little demon. I refer to the one which can't stand it for others to feel good when we feel bad.

But this initial wrath will pass if you keep calm. When it is over, he will be glad that one pair of feet remains firmly on solid ground. In time, you can work this out to a "deal" where he does his best to stay topside when it is your turn to go below.

One reason why you might be tempted to despondency when he is despondent is that you may blame yourself unduly for his bad moods. If you are at fault and you know it you will say so. But groveling in the emotional sloughs of self-criticism is strictly no good when it is *his* black mood and not your doing. You are growing up when you can honestly say, "I will remember that this is *his* problem. I will refuse to punish myself. My job is to keep calm and ready. I will prepare my heart to give him the most mature love I can manage as soon as he gives me the opening."

I have observed some skillful women doing another clever thing. *They get ready for their husband's bad moods before the low ceiling comes down.*

Maybe you can learn your man's weak points and "seed the tornado" to scatter the ugly winds. One of the most successful wives among our friends says that she asks her husband to barbecue her a steak when she feels some inner woe sneaking up on him. She testifies that the combination of a big meal and her accolades to his cooking works wonders for him.

Maybe you should go dancing. Perhaps a long drive in the

moonlight is the right antidote. If he prefers to come home and glower there then put on your best, roll out your dark blue carpet, and let him work it out under his own roof. Some men I know would give their bottom dollar if they could have such a "shelter of a rock from a weary land" in their own home.

If you make enough progress at handling these things together, you might even learn to give each other warning signals. Catherine Anthony says that she and Jim have agreed to this jewel: If he's had a rough day at the office, if he's off his usual cheery base, if the stock market is down, or he lost an account he hoped to get, then Jim wears a red feather in his hat when he comes home. "Warning, dear! This is no evening to present that unexpected bill or to report the broken throttle on the mower!"

There is one thing more you can do. This is, in fact, *the* big curative! It is the one where your mother and I find our most effective remedy. You spell it with four letters: *Talk!*

The phone just rang. It's a couple asking if I can come right now. There are so many husbands and wives who are total strangers to each other in important areas.

So, let's talk about talk in our next letter!

Yours for clearing skies,
Dad

The Bridge of Communication

My dear Karen,

"Are you good at talking things over? Can you discuss your feelings together? Are there certain subjects you must tiptoe around? How good are you at communicating your inmost thoughts with each other?"

Questions such as these are favorites with premarital counselors. Most of the couples I marry assure me that this is one of their strongest points.

But up against their claim put these echoes of common complaints heard often in our work with couples who have been married several years.

> "You know how you feel when the phone rings and nobody answers? That's how I feel!"
>
> "Now please don't tell my husband I said that, will you?" ... "Don't you dare say anything about this to my wife!" ... "What do you mean, discuss it? My wife is a sphinx!"
>
> "He never answers. He only grunts!" ...
>
> "With us, it's like being married to strangers!"

These are exact quotations from the dirges I've heard, and their variations come often to my ears.

What do you suppose happens to the lovers who were so sure of their ability here? There are many answers, so we'll start with this letter and continue through several more, giving attention to an all-important piece of construction which we will call: *The Bridge of Communication!*

1. *Do greet him with gladness when he first comes home.*

One husband made this picturesque statement: "She throws the garbage in my face the first thing when I open the door." Then he went on to explain that she had a knack for saving the worst news of each day and giving him this promptly on his arrival. You will recognize that he was a master with words as he mimicked her patter: "Junior broke the neighbor's bird bath!" ... "That left rear tire on the station wagon is flat again!" ... "Won't you *please* fix my kitchen faucet? I told you five days ago how awful it leaks!" ... "I understand the Watsons are getting a divorce!" ... and so on in woeful detail.

These evil tidings are strictly no good for his homecoming. Occasionally there must be exceptions, but every good meeting for minds will lay certain items aside for later consideration.

Now, here comes an interesting phenomenon about some men. The same male who objects to this treatment may wish to unload *his* trash the minute he arrives. Maybe he picked up the idea somewhere that wives are for listening to the bad and the husbands are for listening to the good.

During your first months together, if he should be one of these, I'd let him get away with it. Obviously, this isn't exactly fair, but be a wise little gal and "play like" that's how you understood it, too.

Turn down the stove if you can, turn the FM to some soothing music, and draw him close. Let your heart be his mourner's bench.

Such gentleness from you in your early days can pave the way for you to teach him later the wisdom of postponing his "Isn't-it-all-just-terrible?" talk.

From what I've seen, it's a good idea to now and then check your words of greeting.

2. *Do set aside time for visiting together.*

A whimsical cartoon in one of our magazines pictured an attractive mother telling her two children their bedtime story. This was the plaintive caption: "Children, your father is about five-foot-ten, dark hair, cute little mustache, well-tanned, and *he is just wild about golf!*"

Every husband should have his hobby, and the same goes for your side. In one of our early letters we discussed time apart from each other as a magnet which will eventually draw you closer to each other. But the land is full of foolish couples whose love has been diverted now until they are "just wild" about something other than their hours together.

So, what can you do about this? Sometimes little remedies bring big changes. You might add a lot to your way of life by working out what you've heard us call our "conversational compacts."

I'm sure you'll remember what a good thing we did at our house when we all agreed to this pledge: "We will save time for loitering at our evening meal. We will share the day's highlights and discuss these together. We will present our 'most interesting things' and vote on matters important to us all."

In one vital marriage I know, the husband and wife have what they call their "little deal." They say, "it turned out to be one of the biggest deals we ever made!" They promised each other that they would take a few minutes at bedtime to share this question, "What was the happiest moment of your life today?"

Other couples have agreed to at least one meal out together each week. They allow for a baby-sitter in their budget and set aside funds for dinner at one of their favorite eating places. Social events with others do not count. These are their moments alone to "focus their souls."

Of course, there will be extreme emergencies which interrupt any covenant you make. But don't let yourselves go so fast, or be so preoccupied, that you fail to notice the sign approaching this bridge. It reads: "The River of Time!"

3. *Do learn all you can about his work.*

A man came to my study one evening to give me a check. It was a tithe of his first royalty on an invention. How about this for an ideal wife?

"This patent which has begun to pay off," he began, "is really not my idea. Grace studied everything she could find about my work. She read and attended lectures. She talked with every expert she could corner. Then one day she said, 'Al, with your brilliant mind'—that's what she said, you see—'I'll bet you could invent an electronic eye to tell the difference between good peas and bad peas while they're still in the pod. This is how I've got it figured.'"

Then he went on to detail the idea. It was over my head *but it wasn't over his!* He went after it with zeal and developed this ingenious device.

This isn't all the story. Measure the woman now against this additional statement: "She made me promise I would never tell anyone where I got the idea. My bosses think I'm really something. They gave me my own private lab to work up some new money-makers. And guess who's helping me most? How could I ever be grateful enough for a woman like Grace?"

Then he handed me their contribution and asked if I would say a prayer for them. So I prayed. With thanksgiving and praise, I prayed that they might continue to be "in tune" with the Infinite for greater things.

They will! A woman like this is a real find for any man. Let's let that suffice for our third "Do!"

"Don'ts" are important also for the traffic of your heart through your lips. Here are three worth remembering:

1. *Don't let your common interests get away.*

Nearly every couple facing marriage has many things which have drawn them together. But sometimes these die a gradual death from other causes than we have mentioned in our "Do's." What's the reason?

One major origin of this demise is when one member tends to dominate the conversation. Rushing madly from secondly to thirdly to fourthly, they suffocate the dialogue with monologue.

Many of us have this tendency. We love the sound of our own words, and we forget that although our voice may ring like a bell to us, it is more like the caw of a crow to the other person who waits and waits to express himself.

Skillful wives I've known seem to have several marks of wisdom at this point: (a) They know many clever little ways to give their men the "you go first" treatment! (b) They "yield the floor" quickly when they see any indication that he has something to say! (c) They learn how to read their husbands for these signals—the raised eyebrow, the slightest movement in the corner of his lips, a furrowed brow, or some special gesture peculiar to him.

It is true that he should make every effort to be attentive to your thoughts. I hope he'll be as wise about this as he expects you to be. But you'll hear his footsteps on your bridge more often if you develop this delicate radar.

If you do this well, those common interests which meant so much at the beginning can grow through the years. Gradually they become a trellis on which your shared words intertwine. This makes your bridge of communication more attractive to you both.

2. *Don't try to impress him with how much you know.*

Jealousy of every kind is dangerous stuff in marriage, and one of its worst forms is mental envy. If he knows things unknown to you, you have discovered a great thing when you can humble your mind to say, "I admire your brains! Teach me!"

Then there will be places where your knowledge supersedes his. With this you must be at your best. Without making a display of it, you can learn the technique which we call "putting the latchstring low enough!"

Do you remember when you and Philip were tots we placed a knob on the screen door low enough for you to reach? It saved two youngsters considerable frustration. The idea came from an elderly guest at our house who wearied of your banging for entrance. His suggestion not only made life easier for you, it also saved many steps for mother and dad.

You have observed how many of the truly great people learn to reduce their brilliance to reachable heights. The same goes for both of you. You must each master the art of lowering the handles to give what you do know and to receive what you don't.

Wise wives remember this—he'll take more pride in his woman's discernments if she never parades hers while she plays up his.

3. *Don't fail to still your lips when you should.*

Actually, this is all we've been saying in our other don'ts, isn't it? We'll probably say it again—and again! The reason for all this repetition is that I see a steady stream of these chattering women as I work with problem marriages.

One group might be labeled "The Interrupters!" This is a common human tendency for many of us. We sit on the edge of our chairs and wait impatiently for an opening. Or sometimes we don't wait! At the first drawing of breath from the other fellow, we seize the floor and tell how it really was or how we know it should be! Since I'm not a lady, I can't tell how it feels from your side, but I have observed that not many of us men go for women who are constantly breaking in on our wisdom.

Another variety of the "ceaseless" might be classified as "Overquestioners!"

The same man who hopes sometime to get in a word, may yearn at other times for nothing more than a peaceful reverie with himself! We all have within us those personal places where our minds are tied in knots, and *we* know the knot is not ready for loosening. Other items require working in private before they can be shaped in correct phrases.

We began our letters on the premise that we do not know everything about each other just because we are married. That concept is worth frequent review.

You *do* have a right to know some things "right this minute!" So does he. But other things will only come across the bridge at their own private pace.

For this reason, to love well is often to wait well.

This could go on and on. But here comes that drummer again! He's sounding his favorite theme—some of the road to heaven must be taken at a slow shuffle!

This is how it is as you develop the art of communication between you. But if you do develop it well, you may come one day to a thrilling experience. This is the great hour when you can commune together in stillness. Marvelous moments these! They need no words. You can drive for miles, sit for long periods, and share your souls in silent conversation. No voice could add to this. All is quiet inside and your hearts are at peace.

Here is a little prayer which I try to remember before every talk and each sermon. It was taught me by a wise professor who knew the value of things said and the worth of the unsaid also. Maybe you'd both like to learn it for your life together:

"Lord, fill my mouth with worthwhile stuff and nudge me when I've said enough!"

Dad

Eyeball-to-Eyeball

My dear Karen,

"Eyeball-to-eyeball" is the shortened version of what your mother and I call: *"Our seven official rules for a good, clean fight."*

The "oneing" of two hearts calls for much billing and cooing. But if you are wise you will get ready for another sound. This is the battle cry! Wherever two red-blooded people are building a home, you'll find occasional spats and, now and then, some fiery encounter.

This news should not blow you down! If you learn how to handle them, these small wars may be just what your marriage needs.

Venting the air in your insides through lips which have learned how to do it can serve a good purpose in you. It may also be good for other people with whom you associate.

If Vincent has a "blowing-off" place behind his own doors he might be more effective at his work. Most occupations these days require strict sublimation of feelings even when a man has every right to "let himself go." A well-kept skirmish procedure at home can be a blessing to him, a blessing to you, and a blessing to his fellow workers. It could even be a secret to his advancement, and, oh, how we love those raises!

Good, clean fighting can be excellent preventive medicine for your common good health. It might prevent headaches, heartaches, and high blood pressure. Ulcers and allergies, moods and nagging, and a whole host of other things you'd like to avoid can be added to this list.

Besides all this, *it's fun if you do it right!* When some couple says, "We've been married 'X' number of years with never a cross word between us," you should know this—it usually means that they have learned some method of laying their differences on the table and talking them out.

If they really *do* live together with the sheepishness of sheep, then they're missing a lot of real living. In one of our churches, the senior-high president was a cute redhead named Delphine. She was asked to present the lesson one night on an Old Testament character. The "ho-hum" attitude with which she began was not at all like Delphine. But before she was done she summed up her trouble with this classic statement, "Kids, I feel sorry for this man. I've hunted through all his stories, and, as nearly as I can figure it, *the poor guy lived a normal life!*"

I wish I could remember who he was. I can't recall even one well-known Bible character in that sad condition. Maybe she missed something. But if she was right then we *should* join in her sympathy!

Life is partly for fun, and part of the fun is working out problems, handling differences, struggling for a meeting of minds, surfacing inner entanglements, and learning how to handle these well.

So roll your guns up on the bridge occasionally and get ready for the zip and tang of facing "eyeball-to-eyeball."

Here now are our "Seven Official Rules for a Good, Clean Fight." We signed them in our souls as affirmations, and we'll give them to you here just as we've enjoyed them for twenty-five years.

1. *Before we begin we must* both *agree that the time is right.*

There is an eager little beaver in nearly everyone which likes to get right on with it when something is needling inside. Then we have other days when it takes all our strength just to go on breathing.

A wise woman learns to purr with the kittens sometimes when she would prefer to scratch with the cats. If he's suffering from "battle fatigue" at the office, this is not a good time. The smart man also learns how to command "Arms Rest!" even if his spleen is ready for venting. Since women have hard days with the children and weeks when they're not up to their best, he too must practice self-control. That little word "*both*" in this rule grows more important as you study it.

You can also learn to read each other's signs that the time is drawing near for getting on with it. That I might have more expert feminine advice for you, I recently asked a small group of women if they would mind sharing with me their husbands' war flags.

Here are four observations which I selected for your musing: "Whenever he begins to swear at the traffic, that's my tip!"—"I can tell something's bothering him when he begins using a whole lot more salt on his food!"—"If he gets unusually fussy about the way his shirts are done, he's getting ready!"—"My man is looking for a fight when he begins complaining about the bills!"

Naturally, these will differ with different men but you can learn Vincent's. Some things better wait. Some things should not wait. Some things might wait too long.

Whatever you do, you *both* better make certain you know the bailiff's two questions, "Is the defendant ready?" and "Is the plaintiff prepared?"

2. *We will remember that our only battle aim is a deeper understanding of each other.*

There are several important gun labels for conversational warfare between husbands and wives who really do care.

"Humility and honesty" will be the theme of a later letter but you'll need these now. Neither of you is "all St. George" and neither of you is "all the dragon."

"Patience" is another requirement. Without it you could tear up more in an hour than it might take weeks to repair.

"Mercy," "Grace," and "Telling the truth in love" should be in your hearts as you shout, "Ready-aim-fire!"

If either of you is to hit the bull's eye you must never forget this: Your main aim is to improve your marriage by deeper understanding!

3. *We will check our weapons often to be sure they're not deadly.*

This follows naturally on the heels of what we've been saying. "The battle unto death" may be all right in its place but its place is not in the home. Here you are shooting down troubles, not firing for funerals!

So be especially careful of the words you hurl when the smoke gets in your eyes.

Right now, I am working to patch up a marriage where they lost their tempers and he made a serious mistake. He shouted in anger, "I *never did* like your darned old freckles anyway!"

She had freckles all over her face, and they were honestly one of the nicest things about her. But they had bothered her since her early teens. He had always told her that he was crazy about them, and I'm sure he was with part of him. But another part was not, and he let that part get out of hand when their fight was at fever pitch.

We're making some progress. He has apologized a thousand times. Yet for a long time there will be that sneaky little worry in her mind, "Does he *really* like my freckles as he has always vowed he did? Or was he telling the truth when he lost control?"

"Sadism" is bad in any form, and one of its worst forms is to throw up to others those things they can *never* change.

Even the mildest criticism is best handed over softly. When it is hurled in rage it may bring retorts which might add nothing and take away much.

We all have within us a defense mechanism which comes roaring out of its corner when we are censored! Some men learn much from their women about self-control. If you remain master of your tongue, even when he doesn't, he may emerge from this battle with a new respect for a wonderful wife who knows what not to say when!

Another weapon to lay aside permanently is the overused phrases which have become so tiresome that they automatically bring bad reactions. One successful couple I know says that they have agreed to delete "never" and "always" from their battle vocabulary. "You are *never* home on time!" Or "You *always* put the children first!" ignite fuses for them which lead to trouble. So they have wisely decided to eliminate these triggering words. You'll soon learn your own "loaded" phrases and do as they've done.

Now comes a paradox! We have said that there are times when no answer is the best answer. But at other times it may be worse *to say nothing* than *to say something!* The utter absence of any utterance from the lady he loves may be one of the loudest noises a man ever heard if he's dying for her to break her silence!

So study rule three and use it smartly. The swords you swing on this "battle of the bridge" must be cut of the stuff which bends and gives. Your cannon balls should be more like snowballs than great balls of fire.

4. *We will lower our voices instead of raising them.*

This is the one rule of our seven which was built into our courtship before we were married. It came, as so many good things of our love, from out of your mother's quiet. In my stormy background we "hollered" when our ire was up, and the volume went higher with the increasing ire.

I have told you how I fell in love with your mother's voice before I had seen her face. She was reciting one day in our high school class. It was a large group of students, and I was staring out the window wondering whether this particular sophomore might start the big game.

Then, like a soft angelus to my ears, came the sound of deep peace. I looked to its source and right then I made a vow. If I ever began to think much of girls, this was the one I'd begin to think much of first.

You know the rest. When we began our dating I sense what Shakespeare meant when he said, "Her voice was ever soft, gentle, and low, an excellent thing in woman!"

But as with all sweethearts, the first hour of anger arrived, and I began the customary procedure. So she stopped me in my vocal tracks and explained that she knew a better way. "Why don't we agree," she said from her inner stillness, "that from now on when we fuss we'll lower our voices one octave rather than raising them two?"

It's been an awesome struggle. But that's how it is. For a husband to tone down his volume may require the strictest discipline. The same for some women.

5. *We will never quarrel in public nor reveal private matters.*

We belonged to a group in one of our churches which included a pair of bloodhounds. These were "people bloodhounds," a husband-wife pair who were constantly nosing about for each other's negligibles.

Example: He would be reciting the happy memories of their vacation trip. She sniffed along behind him scenting for a mistake. Then it happened. He made *the* horrible error! Recalling the pleasures of their two weeks away he said, "On the first Tuesday it rained, so we stayed in the cabin and played cards!"

Now we go!

"*No! No! No!* Don't you remember, darling, on Tuesday we drove over the mountain. *Wednesday* was the day it rained!"

So the war was on.

"It was *too* Tuesday; it *had* to be Tuesday because, etc., etc.!" Before long we were hearing the full record of Monday, Thursday, Friday, Saturday, Sunday. Then they were marching their soldiers into the second week!

In this group there was a delightfully rugged cattleman whom we called "Big Ed." He was mighty in many ways and one of those was with blasting words when his boilers were going inside. With secret cheers from all of us he roared in their ears, "*Why don't you two do your dirty laundry at home?*"

That is a good question with only one answer. All private rubbing and scrubbing should be done in its place—and its place is in private!

There is one more subpoint to our rule. This is our agreement that we will never fire at each other publicly when we are *not* together. I have known very few men who could readily forgive their wives for criticizing and complaining behind their backs.

Be sure to tell Vincent that women differ little from men right here!

So underscore rule five with a heavy red pencil.

6. *We will discuss an armistice whenever either of us calls "halt."*

Notice the wording, "We will *discuss* an armistice!" Some men are quitters by nature, and some women run up the white flag too soon! With us it requires a unanimous vote of two before we finally sign the truce. Sometimes silence is not golden. It may be a pale shade of yellow.

If you agree to these rules, then a sense of fair play is an absolute must all the way through to the end. Without good sportmanship on both sides you can't have the kind of "good, clean fight" which our rule-label bears.

Yet, as we have seen, some things in marriage can go either way. Some men want to stay up all night and push the adversary around!

How *can* you end it if you want to quit and he wants to continue? Here is one move for cease-fire which seldom fails for us. It goes like this—"I'm *beginning* to see what you meant! But I'll need some time to think this over. *Please, let's make up now so I can consider awhile how you could be right!*" (He could be, you know!)

If this doesn't get through, your marriage may be sicker than you think! Perhaps you need help from experts outside to go far down inside and settle more serious problems than rules such as these could ever cure.

7. *When we have come to terms we will put it away until we* both *agree it needs more discussing.*

A healthy union requires that you never forget some things and never remember others. Wedlock must have its lock boxes. In some of these you put certain items and throw the key away. Others you keep for later opening.

Did you notice that "both" in this rule also? If one "eyeball" glowers unduly at the "wait-a-whiles" you will do well to talk it over and maybe take out the problem for review.

One of the most infinite understandings in any husband-wife relationship is that *you can still love each other even if there are things you don't exactly like around here!*

We recently heard a luncheon speaker make the statement that no married couple should ever go to bed without talking out *everything* between them. He based his claim on the words of Paul, "Let not the sun go down on your wrath!"

We had no opportunity to talk to the man after his address but I wonder if he really meant *everything!* Paul's words sound ideal but the trouble is that, without interpretation, they are only headed in the general direction of truth.

Some scholars argue that Paul had been married. Others insist he had not. But whether he had or hadn't, if you will study all his letters you will come to the conclusion that he knew what he was about!

It was this same Paul who taught us that people filled with the right spirit will be marked by the fruits of "love, joy, peace, long-suffering, gentleness, goodness, faith, meekness, temperance!" Who could talk their way through to all of these before one day's sun goes over the hill?

So keep at it. Keep working. Keep resting. Keep trusting. Keep firing. Keep surrendering. Keep these things for later. Keep those locked forever. Keep talking. Keep listening. Keep going.

You won't reach the loftiest ranges by nightfall! But you won't need to!

If you keep giving this day all the love your hearts can produce, then tomorrow will keep giving you a larger and greater love.

For lovers who keep on keeping on with their love there is never an end to the glories of marriage.

Keep up the fight right,
Dad

"I'm Sorry, Honey"

My dear Karen,

The three most important words in marriage, next to "I love you," may be the humble little admission, "I'm sorry, honey!"

We have already dealt with the fact that living together in perfect harmony is more ideal than real. Even toward the one we love most there may be flashes of hatred. You will take a sensible attitude toward this. Perhaps those angry words needed to "surface." Maybe they cleared subterranean chambers to make room for more love.

Since apology is a prime ingredient in marriage, we'll give this letter to three thoughts I hope will be helpful.

1. *Some people find it difficult to express regret.*

One wife, married to a holier-than-thou husband, gave this sad witness in our consultation together: "David is *always* on the Lord's side, and it is so hard to get along with a man who is *always* on the Lord's side!"

These are tough men to live with. It is also rough for husbands whose wives comport themselves as self-ordained saints. You will sense immediately that here is another place where the problem could have long roots. Perhaps he was taught that remorse of any kind is one form of weakness. Maybe he offered an apology once and it was rejected. Possibly you can help him ferret out the reason and set him free of one more bothersome hanger-on from his childhood.

You will do well to examine your quarreling for signs that you might be the guilty party this time. If you are over-defending yourself to yourself; if you are continually whipping the villain around the block with your thoughts; or feeling sorry for yourself; or mountain climbing over molehills; or sounding like a commanding officer whenever you talk; or indulging in any one of your favorite rationalizations, then this may be your day for confession. An Old Testament prophet gives us a word for those times when we "status quo" our defenses and refuse to budge: "In vain dost thou use many medicines; there is no healing for thee!"

We have been over this rocky road before in our letters, so let's move along now with this chant of the great women: "*Bigness may never begin unless it begins with me!*"

Even if it is *all* his fault, which isn't likely, you can patch up a quarrel and still keep your self-respect! If he refuses to be honest, you can be honest enough to say, "I'm sorry we quarreled. Forgive me for anything I said which I shouldn't have said. There are so many things I like about you. I appreciate your love more than anything in the world, and it makes me feel just awful when we are out of sorts with each other."

Without being a phony you can make every effort to square the thing from your side. Then if he still persists, you have at least prepared your soul to receive him heartily when he is ready. It is a sick man who forever rejects the sincere "I'm waiting to love you" message from an honest woman's heart.

Apology usually requires that the most mature member of your duo make the first move. Some marital experts say that the secret to success in the home is to change the customary fifty-fifty sharing of everything to sixty-forty. They tell us that when both members of the union are willing to go more than half way, this couple has it made. Their wisdom applies particularly to expressing regret. We'll hope you both can develop the stretch to go more than half way.

2. *Regrets and humor go well together.*

Some anonymous sage suggests that we take a long step forward when we can conjugate this verb:

I am a joke
Thou art a joke
He is a joke
We are jokes
Ye are jokes
They are jokes

It helps put our soul in order when we start the conjugation with "*I* am a joke!"

Now comes across the hills of yesterday another fact to remember. Your grandmother was fond of saying, "Don't you ever forget there are two kinds of funny. There is 'funny ha-ha' and 'funny peculiar' and you better know which is which."

This fits many places, and one of these is in the close interchange of marital expression. Excessive laughter may indicate more hysteria than good health! Some stages of marriage are no place for comedy.

Smiles are of many kinds too. You will be alert to which one of your many faces is exactly right when. Never fake the act if the play calls for a solid touch of the real thing!

But whenever a couple learns how to laugh and smile and make merry over their mistakes, a wonderful thing happens in their home. High heaven has special clean-up squads which respond to these signals. They come to sweep away the broken pieces and give that marriage a fresh beginning.

3. *Apology is one of those places in marriage where "Who did it?" or "Why did he?" or "How could she?" isn't as important as "What is the quickest way of making things right again?"*

Mr. Reed taught me a great thing. The little town where I grew up was an ideal spot for boys who loved water. One day the river authority announced a canoe race. The contest was upstream in a section which none of our gang knew. We had plenty of time to prepare, so naturally we examined the course with care and practiced many hours. Mr. Reed lived along the banks where we played regularly, and he was our friend. In one of our evening visits I was complaining about the jagged stones and boulders up there. He listened to my sad story for a time. Then he stopped me with these words of wisdom, "Son," he advised, "you'll never win by fussing about the rocks. Quit worrying about them and *learn where the channels are!*"

That is a fair word for lovers. Let's say he did start it. Or maybe *you* are the guilty party. Possibly neither one can remember its origin. But *where* it began isn't the major matter. What counts most is *when* it is settled? With some things of love "the sooner, the better," and that rule writes itself here with a heavy hand!

Tennyson in *Idylls of the King* puts it well:

It is the little rift within the lute
That by and by may make the music mute!

So, if this is one of those days, go right this minute to the phone and dial his number. In your tenderest voice let the love in your heart pour itself out. Joy breaks through an outburst of new glory, and you achieve real dignity when you discharge the obligation of your errors with these three next most important words in marriage: "*I'm sorry, honey!*"

With proper apologies,
Dad

P.S. I thought you might be interested to hear that we are working on David, the chap who is "always on the Lord's side!" I think we're making some progress. He is beginning to rearrange his pomposity. If he continues his improvement, one day I will be able to remind him that it was Moses, not David, who brought down the laws of God from Mt. Sinai!

The "H" Twins: Humility and Honesty

My dear Karen,

My favorite "Timid Soul!" cartoon shows Caspar Milquetoast standing on the corner in a driving rain. Water is running down the brim of his hat and, although he shivers in misery, he has finally mustered his courage to say, "If that fellow doesn't come in another forty-five minutes, *he can just go and borrow the money from somebody else!*"

Humility is often pictured like this. But to be truly humble, in the finest sense, has nothing to do with cringing before others and groveling our way through life.

One of my Quaker friends uses a term which closes in on its true meaning. When he has been "put down" by life or people or circumstances, he says with a smile, "My soul has been 'meeked!'"

I have heard lengthy discussions, read numerous sermons, and studied the writing of the scholars as they expound on what is meant by the phrase, "Blessed are the meek!" Their interpretations vary from something like poor Caspar to potent phrases which ring with power.

Tracing it back to its original usage, I get the feeling that *to be meek means to face up to the difference between what we are and what we ought to be.*

The greatest people I know are rich with this kind of humility. The same goes for the finest marriages. You will add much to your life with each other if you can say, "Blessed are the couples who are humble and honest, for they will reach a higher love!"

Several fine things happen when you live by this beatitude. Courage to analyze yourselves, grace to apologize sincerely, patience to hold your tongues when you should, the ability to lead each other down the hall to the mirror—these are but a few of the good things which "the 'H' twins" bring along if you invite them into your home.

Let's take a look at two ugly items which will be discouraged from knocking so often at your doors if your souls are being "meeked" together.

"*Gossip*" is one of these. There is a familiar adage which goes, "Small minds discuss people; average minds discuss happenings; great minds discuss ideas!"

Naturally, there will be times when your talk centers on folks and days when it shares events. But you do well to check your conversation often to be sure it isn't blowing bits of outside dust and dirt into the center of your thoughts.

Judgment and "jury duty" have their place. So do censorship and criticism. But their major place is not in your home.

Whether men are as guilty as women here is open to debate. Many of us men *will* have some accounting to do at this point.

But you can develop some clever preventives if you dedicate your tongues to constructive rather than destructive talk.

A card club of my acquaintance did an interesting thing. The lady who reported this to me said, "Not one of our girls would steal money. We wouldn't steal things either. Yet we had fallen into the habit of carelessly stealing somebody's good name without thinking."

Then one brave soul dared to speak up. Since these really were women of character, they got the message and faced facts. As a corrective measure they framed this delightful wisecrack and put it in a prominent place where everyone would see it during their play:

"I wouldn't say anything about
her unless I could say something
good—and, boy, is this good!"

According to them it works wonders and there is a refreshing new spirit in their fellowship. If all occupants of every home would go and do likewise, this might be an air-purifier well worth its price!

Humility and honesty may be difficult to achieve partially because it is easier to nose about in somebody else's basement than to clean up your own soot and ashes.

If you persist you won't mature to the greatness in you. When you do down "their" stairs you yourself go down. If you turn your steps upward to their better points you go up. Here is one of those universal laws which works no other way.

To allow yourselves this "we-are-good-but-they-are-not-so-good" attitude will eventually dirty up your bridge of communication and make it unattractive to both.

"*Nagging*" is among the major gripes heard in my study. For some reason, more husbands bring me this complaint than women. Again, I'm not certain that wives do it more than their men, but I'm sure of this—one way to keep him loving you is to avoid carping and harping of any kind.

Those who overdo here may need to travel back down the paths of their personal histories to discover some reasons for their censorious natures. Perfectionism is one of the most common sources. Whenever a child is brought up by adults whose spirit is "nothing but the best from you will satisfy us," that child may develop a pointed tongue. A severe upbringing which ingrains unnatural standards is almost certain to create dissatisfaction with everything and everybody.

Men who must live with women of this temperament do not become more teachable. They only build up their defenses that much higher and finally erect soundproof barriers in their ears. Or, if their hearing apparatus is not equipped to do this, they stay away from the juggernaut of charges and countercharges which their marriage has become. Working overtime when they don't need to, excessive drinking, philandering, and, finally, their lawyer's office may be havens of rest compared to the wild winds of their woman's words!

One such man described his wife with this damning statement: "She'd make an excellent district attorney! She has her process-servers out for my faults, and she keeps them working seven days a week, twenty-four hours a day!"

That's a pitiful statement, isn't it? I regret that there are others to match it in every hamlet and city. So, when you find yourself even slightly inclined in this direction, stop right there and turn the process-servers inside you.

"The 'H' twins" will bring their own cleaning equipment if you can give them access to every nook and cranny. But these fact-finding crews have an uncomfortable way of always starting with "number one" or they refuse to start. Eventually, they may move their buckets and mops to the other side of the union but don't ask them to commence there. They never do!

"*My* soul has been meeked!" is how my Quaker friend puts it. I trust you'll have the wisdom and grace to join those feminine lovelies who know that he has his words in their right order.

If you had the wings of an angel you'd probably be ready for heaven and, though we all hope to make it eventually, we're more likely to arrive there when we say, and mean it, "My soul, *thou* ailest here and here!"

From one side of your family you come out of stock which found it terribly hard to open the inner box and face the devils there. But from the other side you have learned that there is no other road to inner peace.

This is tough stuff we're dealing with here. May you have the largeness of soul to *examine yourself first* in humility and honesty.

Yours for true meekness together,
Dad

P.S. I just remembered this one woman who said: "I was operating under the delusion that I needed a new husband. Then one day it occurred to me that perhaps my husband needed a new wife!"

Getting Through to the Real Self

My dear Karen,

It is very important for you to understand this about men. Most of their day is spent in an impersonal world.

In certain professions what the man *does* matters more than how he really *feels*. In some jobs what he *produces* for his company is more important in their eyes than *how he thinks*.

Modern business is so developed that the person is often eclipsed behind the almighty dollar, and a man's real self may be seriously repressed.

Because of this, a man will do almost anything for a woman who can get through to the inner man.

Here is an example of what I mean. You will not remember this because you were little.

This leader in the church, father of two grown daughters, gave up his wife and married the elevator girl.

I wasn't the only one horrified. The whole town was undone when he sold his successful business and moved to another state to start over. It seemed for a time in our community that there was nothing else going on in the world except this.

But I want to pass on some lines he shared with me when he came to say goodbye. We had been the best of friends, and we could talk heart-to-heart. When it came the moment for some word of explanation, this is the way he put it:

"Charlie, I don't expect you to understand, but let me tell you how it started. One day we were alone in the elevator going up. Just before she opened the door at my floor she laid her hand on my arm and said, "Please don't think me forward, but I want you to know I think you are the kindest man in this whole building. For four years I've watched you tip your hat to the ladies and smile. Only you do it differently from other men. With you it's more as if it came from your heart. I just wanted to say thank you for being what you are.'"

Then he went on to explain that over the weeks they began to visit and he discovered what she meant. She had been married twice before and she told him, "Both these men *treated me as if I were a thing*." That, he said, was the statement which lit the fires because that's how he felt about himself. He had been a faithful husband, and I knew it. He had been a good father, and I knew this also. That he had been a fine provider the whole town could see.

But there was one thing lacking and this is how he described it: "My wife didn't love me *for me!* She loved me *for herself!* She 'used' me so my daughters did it, too. I didn't realize until I met another empty heart such as mine *how much it means to be loved because you are you!*"

That's what the man said. He gave up status, investments, leadership, a secure future. He turned his back on all this for an elevator girl who got through to share the real self with him.

I never could discuss it with the forsaken wife. We had been friends, too, but she pulled down the shades on her heart now and refused to talk about it. He said no more than these few lines I've shared with you.

But I can pass on a few things I've picked up through the years since that first shocking experience. I've seen it happen many times, and there are certain things which *will not* be conducive to your man's opening his full self to you. In our fourth letter we discussed the freedom factor which will work toward his unfolding. We've considered honesty and apology as additional helps toward self-disclosure. We'll see to others later. But right now, I'd suggest you eliminate three words from your marriage and keep them erased if you hope to get through all the way.

1. *"Ridicule!"*

Of course, he'll have some wild ideas. Every thinker does. But when he comes up with one, hear him out in rapt attention. This may represent something which came to him in a flash at the office. He's been asking himself, "Have I made a brilliant discovery, or are there 'bugs' here which I don't see?" He'd like to be sure before he presents it to his superiors. He knows that men often judge men by their ability to consider every angle before they go off half-cocked.

Let's say it again! Most of us husbands are required to live behind some partial facade in our positions. We see things which we know are true. We see others we know are wrong. Yet "politics" or "timing" or "expediency" may call for sublimation. We also sense that though we check things dozens of times in the secret of our minds we may miss some errors which show up when our thoughts are expressed aloud. All this makes home that much more attractive if we can share our repressed thoughts knowing that they will get a full hearing with no hint of derision.

So, let him talk even if he is far out in left field and you know it. Don't cut him off too soon. Perhaps he'll discover the flaw for himself in free expression. A mature man gets a real thrill from catching on to his own loose thinking. But if he doesn't see and you do, pace yourself now! There will be plenty of time later for you to bring him carefully back where the facts are.

You can laugh *with* him. You can tell him he's the funniest in fun. But never laugh *at* the things he shares with you until he laughs first. Ridicule in small doses or large will clam any man eventually.

2. *"Overfastidiousness!"*

This is a long word and it would take too much time to spell it out in all its meanings. The reason is that some men like one type of neatness and some another. But my observation is that the perfectionist wife is generally heading for trouble.

This applies both to keeping the house and keeping yourself.

No home is likely to represent the acme of loveliness for a man unless there is something here which seems to say, "Come! Let down, way down!" If the whole place is so impeccably kept that it smacks of stiffness, you may discourage his self-disclosure.

Same goes for you. The "china-doll-mustn't-touch" look is for china dolls. It is true that women are to admire and behold in their loveliness. You'll want him to be proud of your clothes and the way you wear them. Cleanliness of garment and person is also of prime importance, as any girl knows who has eyes for the ads or ears for commercials. So, both in public and for him alone, you'll keep yourself with these things in mind. But the well-groomed woman wears something else with her fresh garments and her cologne. It is that subtle invitation which seems to say, "Come touch me! Take me in your arms!"

This is an art to be learned. It varies with each wife because each husband has his own peculiar likes and dislikes. But it is a wise woman who knows that every man is equipped, both body and soul, with a subconscious radar which seeks some place to let himself go.

3. *"Pushiness!"*

Most husbands also have something inside which automatically erects barriers against the wife who is forever pointing out how much better his friends are doing in the economic world. So, Joe did get to be vice-president! Maybe Vincent doesn't want to do it the way Joe did it! Maybe he doesn't want it—period! Praise him for his accomplishments, but don't wave continually before him the honors of others.

There is a secret gnawing in the heart of any man who feels that he is constantly measured not on his own merits but against the merits of others. Excessive pushing from a woman is one sure "detacher" in marriage. Few males will let down freely in the presence of the "drive-drive-drive" female.

The same thing goes if you shove him around socially until he is out of character. If, during the day, he feels that he must live with a mask for prudence' sake, then he will all the more appreciate friends who feel "natural" and allow him to feel the same.

Evenings and weekends and "free" hours have a special meaning to most men. Of course, they're precious for women, too. Whether being a housewife calls for as much role-playing as that of the breadwinner may be open to discussion. But there is no debating the fact that the man who must live most of his working time in partial cover-up will be grateful for a wife who understands his predicament and provides him a place to be his true self.

One of the challenges we face often in life is to discover the fine line between enough and too much. This is true in these three things.

You must work for an atmosphere where you can tell the whole truth. But this generally comes only after you have proven yourself a sounding-board which never gives off one hint of ridicule.

You will make every effort to keep your house and yourself tidy and clean. But you won't overdo it.

You are wise to let him have a big say in what you belong to, who you go with, and what he can do without your hammering comparison to the accomplishments of others.

This creation of true person-to-person transparency is another of the big things which marriage is about.

It will not come easily! Breaking up the protective crusts we have built around us may be slow business. Sometimes it is painful. Because this is true, there will be times of inner resistance from each side. But don't let these continue too long. It is good to constantly measure your progress and make certain that your opening to each other is moving in the direction of increasing revelation.

You better believe it, my darling daughter—a man will do almost anything for a woman with whom he can learn to share his real self.

With high hopes for getting through,
Dad

The Baby and the Muscle Man

My dear Karen,

The concept of "Papa, the strong protector" and "Mama, the clinging vine" is a favorite theme for melodrama. But in real life it's like the song with the murderous grammar—"'Tain't necessarily so!"

You will be wise to remember that your husband has a little boy in his makeup somewhere. This may be one of those things you can't trace back to its origin. Or maybe you can.

One day I had a frantic call from a desperate father. He pompously announced that I must see his son at once. Things had been going from bad to worse. They needed help "right this very minute, by gad!" Junior was "raising hell at home, raising hell at school, raising hell all over the place." (I'm quoting this father, see?)

So we cleared the calendar, and Junior turned out to be one of the biggest fourteen-year-olds ever to plunk himself down in any pastor's study.

The father introduced us. No response! Next, he admonished his young one with great vigor, "Tell the man what's troubling you, son!" No response.

This pop-to-pop monologue continued for another try, and another, and another, and—then the light! It flashed long enough for me to see this: I would never know whether this monster was deaf and dumb unless we could unload father.

So in my sternest voice I said, "Will you step into the library for a few minutes, please? I'd like to speak with your son in private."

At last we were alone.

It would be more in the interest of accurate reporting if I said *I* was alone!

Though Junior was free to open his mouth and release all his pent-up emotion to "the man," he said not a word.

Quite by accident I began fingering the gold football on my watch chain. I often do this when I'm contemplating the right move.

Then suddenly the dam gates opened. I never did understand all he said that time. But after considerable babbling he came through distinctly minus the gibberish.

"I hate footballs. I'm never going to like footballs, and *will you please stop playing with that awful football?*"

To cut across a long series of visits and many months, let's turn to the last chapter for a peek at the "whodunit" pages.

You guessed it! The real villain was that pushy, pushy pop.

When we finally made a breakthrough on the adult side of the problem, dad confessed that he had been a frustrated football player in his own high school days. (You must not blame the coaches. For good teamwork, everyone *has* to shut up in the huddle to hear the signals.)

So he was inwardly ashamed of his failure. He played it like an old record—"I've been trying to make an athlete out of him since he was three. That's how lots of the stars got their start, you know. But all he does is sit around the house and eat. Never does anything constructive. Besides, he needs the exercise. You agree, don't you, that athletics are good for young boys? I had a talk with the coach and he said this son of mine would be a cinch for all-conference if he cared even a little. He could go to State and get him a scholarship. Then they pay big bonuses in the pros, you know. You've got to remember things like that!—" and so on *ad nauseam.*

Right there father put his big mouth to the real trouble, didn't he? Junior did *not* care "even a little." He had never cared "even a little."

But the story has one happy phase to its ending. Junior did care about one thing, and you'll be surprised when I tell you that he's playing a big part this Friday night. It's not on the football team. He is one of the school's star actors in the senior play. *That's* what he wanted—drama!

What became of the villain? I am pleased to report that two or three psychiatrists, numerous doctor bills, and a few years later father seems to have caught on to one fact. It costs to keep your mouth in high gear all the time.

He isn't completely cured, and the doctor warns that perhaps he never will be. But at least he's changed his tune to something Junior can live with. Today, pop is proclaiming in the streets that "the Hollywood scouts are rumored to be on hand this very Friday. And, by gad, do you know why they're coming? It's to see my Junior, that's why. They pay big money for actors, you know." … et cetera, et cetera.

I have been glad to see father and son sitting side by side in church these last few weeks. His current psychotherapist *is* a dandy! For years this sad dad could not attend divine service with his family. He could sing, and read the litanies, and such as that. But even a poor sermon takes at least twenty minutes and—oh, shucks! You get the point!

Junior wanted to grow up *his* way, and his dad wouldn't let him. This fourteen-year-old giant wasn't really raising all that hell. But you know who was!

There are many ways to raise people, several ways to raise arguments, and one sure way to raise hell. This is to pressure someone near you into doing it your way, by gad, or else!

So there will be times when Vincent will wish to go back to his childhood and live it over again. He'll want to play like he is a little boy.

This is mostly subconscious. Perhaps he doesn't even realize that some part of him was forced out of infancy too soon. (I'm doing some psychological reading by a famous authority who holds that every person on earth struggles sometimes to get back into the womb where life was warm and free from care.)

Some of this is over my head but the part I can understand makes sense. I'm sure it will also have meaning for you. I hope it will because you must allow your husband now and then to put his head in your lap and be thoroughly mothered.

Now, let's talk about muscles. I've never had sufficient time with the head doctor who works on Junior's dad to ask if his wife knew anything about the male ego and how to assuage it.

It wouldn't be fair to blame her anyway. She may have given her very best and not even reached first base. But you will if you teach yourself that sometimes your little boy wishes to step stage-forward as the big, brave man. At these moments he wants you to be "oohing" and "aahing" as you behold all that hair on his chest. He prefers that you swoon a bit in tribute to his biceps and triceps.

Whenever you sense him getting ready for this act, run quick for the soapbox and place it firmly under his feet. Sit there before him with stars in your pretty eyes. Give him the "what-would-I-ever-do-without-you-to-protect-me" treatment. Praise God every time this happens and encourage him to exercise the Tarzan calling to his mate from within.

When we started we stated that this kind of stuff makes excellent script for melodrama. But a little of it also goes well in the real-life drama of love between a wise wife and the lucky man who has one.

Chekhov warned that his plays would be exasperating to the public unless they clearly understood his purpose. His responsibility as a playwright, he said, was only to state the problem. It was up to this audiences to work out their own solutions.

It is unfortunate perhaps that we come to some points in these letters where I must bid adieu like Chekhov.

This is one of those places. I can tell you how it is with men. I can tell you that you must learn these secrets. But, not being a woman, that's all I can tell you.

Since we have now reached a dead end, let's close this particular letter with a beatitude. We'll call this, "Beatitude of a Fortunate Male."

Blessed is the man with a wife who admires her husband for the might of his manhood, but coddles him now and then as a mother comforteth her child.

Yours for some "oohs" and "aahs" plus the maternal instinct,

Dad

Sex Is a Sacrament

My dear Karen,

On that first night when he signs "Mr. and Mrs." to the hotel register, you are entering a physical relationship which we hope will be "out of this world" in more ways than one.

Sex is a sacrament. What goes on between you bodily that night and through the years to come is one of God's precious gifts to his own.

I hope you will come to understand that this part of life is not a duet. It is a trinity. You are really having a relationship with a wise Creator who made your bodies different for his purposes.

So, begin your sex life together on the premise that this is God's love you are sharing here. This is beautiful. This is holy. This is sacred.

When it reaches its best between you, it bursts in heavenly raptures you never knew were hidden within.

It will probably take some doing from both parties to get things started on such a platform. For one thing, society hasn't helped you. You have seen cheap sex in the movies and read it in books. You have heard it vulgarized in off-color stories. You have reviewed its brutal headlines in the papers. It has been displayed before you in advertisements for deodorants and dance halls, macaroni and mascara, soft drinks, shaving lotion, tires, trucks, cigars, cigarettes, and cigarillos.

Now, suddenly, you are expected to lift all this subliminal exposure up to the high level where it belongs? The answer is, of course, same song, next verse—it will take time and it will take effort on your part.

This will not happen all at once, and this is where so many couples make their first serious mistake. They assumed that marriage would automatically bring them where the blessed are. This is simply not so, and you'll be prepared best if you understand that building a heavenly sex life is one of the goals toward which your mating moves. Sometimes its pace is slower than you would like. Occasionally it takes a nice leap forward. Now and then it reaches a plateau. Then it gets moving once more. But, whatever the cadence, it does take time.

Another reason why you might have difficulty touching the stars immediately could be traced to whatever guilt-conscience you bring into your union. This may be some old slip which you thought you had safely buried. These ghosts have a way of pushing over tombstones at the most inappropriate time and leering, "Remember me?"

Or it might be that your courting habits have produced an anxiety you'll find hanging on when it should go away. During your engagement period, you may even have fallen into the practice of quarreling as a release from sexual tension. I have known some married couples who kept right on fussing out of habit when they no longer needed this outlet. You will be alert to all this and remember that it may take a while for official news of the wedding to get all the way through to your inner tribunal. You can help each other with these things. In gentleness and understanding, by patience and tenderness, you make your bed and lie in it for better things in the days to come.

There might even be other reasons why sex is somewhat less than sensational all at once. Sometimes there are unfortunate childhood memories to be overcome. Perhaps certain false impressions were picked up at an early age and have never been clarified. But most of your neurotic repressions will give way gradually provided that you (a) are honest with each other and (b) "love one another with a pure heart fervently."

(You are well aware that there are sources of professional help for those who reach an impasse after giving it their all. But don't bother your pretty head about this sort of thing right now. I've come to appreciate Vincent for many reasons and one of these is his innate soft touch where it matters. It matters right here, so be grateful for sex and let yourself go.)

Let's go back now to where we started. Sex is a sacrament. It is communion of the highest kind. For you, it is communion between Vincent and Karen. It is communion with life at its virile best. But, above all, it is communion with the Lord who created human bodies for other purposes than reproduction of the species alone.

Sex is tapping the deep-flowing rhythms of the universe. It is uniting with the same power which turns the earth in its orbit, pumps sap to the top of the tree, sets out the stars at night, moves water down the river, brings two hearts to stand one day and read life's meaning in each other's eyes. In this phase of marriage, you are actually tuning-in to the creative processes which are far greater than ever man might have done on his own.

In the first chapter of our Bibles there is the beautiful story of our creation. It was obviously written by some ancient wise man to give us the good news that we are not mere accidents going somewhere to happen.

Before this initial chapter of life's most sacred writing has ended, it tells us that in his perfectly marvelous way of doing things the Creator included this wonder of wonders—"male and female created he them." If you will read that chapter again you will note this majestic observation in the closing verse: "*And God saw everything that he had made, and behold, it was very good.*"

Your mother and I can witness firsthand to the truth of this all-inclusive statement. I have counseled with many other husband-wife combinations who would heartily join this song of praise to the Lord who reviewed with pleasure all that he had done.

And among the best of his good things is sex at its best,

Dad

Sexual Differences, Male and Female

My dear Karen,

They say that no two people in the world are alike. Most of us do have two eyes, one nose, a specified number of teeth, five fingers on each hand, and certain other things in common. Yet the statement is true if you take into account all that goes into the making of each individual life.

This will become increasingly obvious as you ponder the truth that no two people have been raised in the same way. Environments differ so much that inevitable variances are part of the background in even the most compatible marriages.

Likewise, heredity factors have shaped him in one pattern and fashioned her from quite a different mold.

Then, in addition to all this, there is another important point for your agenda. There are some distinct differences between men and women just because that's how they were created in the first place.

For example, man is likely to be objective and abstract. Woman is generally subjective and concrete. Man's world of creativity and occupational involvement tends to center his attention outside the home. Woman's most important goings-on will probably focus more on the family.

Because this is true, it is easier for most men to interpret their world in an impersonal manner. Some of us have learned the hard way that women often take things more personally than men.

They forgot to teach us this in school, and it was their mistake. Those of us who work closely with both genders soon find out that you can level with most men and they level back, and then you go drink coffee together as the best of friends. But working with women requires an altogether different set of gears. Many a neophyte (I speak from experience) has stripped some very important cogs in the machinery before he caught on to the difference.

Happy marriage depends in part on making allowances for these essential variances. You can even learn to appreciate such things and let them complement each other in your union.

This will also save you many tears when he doesn't immediately share your enthusiasm for the new drapes or become as overjoyed as you are about baby's first tooth. You also do well to remember these innate divergencies when he brings home some worry from the office and sits with that far-away look in his eye. You might be taking personally something which isn't even remotely related to what you are thinking. What you interpret as a slight on his part may be only a reflection of his being a man and your being a woman.

Now, let's relate this to your sex life.

For many couples, sex begins with general disappointment, moves on to become recurrently disruptive, and at last is quite insipid. Some of these muddled marriages got that way because husband and wife never faced up to this truth—there are some natural biological differences between male and female.

What are they?

1. *Sex probably has deeper meanings to the woman than it does to her man.*

On first thought this may surprise you.

Many a wife in consultation has said things such as this: "It seems that all my husband ever thinks about is sex. He interprets every move I make as a mating move. *Do all* men figure *all* of life by sex symbols *all* the time?"

When you examine this sort of thing carefully you observe an important fact. Man's seeming obsession with sex does not prove that it means more to the male than female. On the contrary, it may mean the opposite. His sex drive is more of a surface, physical thing. Yours is likely to be much deeper, a matter of spirit and soul. He is more easily aroused. Your stirrings come from farther away inside yourself.

One sweet little wife said something to me I'd like to share with you. She, too, had been awed at the apparently insatiable sex appetite of her husband. Unfortunately it was also obvious that he was a clumsy clod in his approaches.

So we discussed this difference-in-the-sexes theme and then she said wistfully: "I had always thought that sex begins at breakfast. A few tender words to start things off would mean so much. Then perhaps a phone call sometime during the day. Some endearments exchanged when he comes home and maybe some help with the supper dishes. Talking things over after the children are in bed. Exchanging ideas. Discussing what we've been doing during the day. A love pat here and a few kisses at the right time. I guess I've had the wrong idea. I thought maybe sex could begin at breakfast, build up during the day, and then explode in bed at night!"

The facts are that she is one hundred percent correct in her analysis of how it ought to be. She couldn't have said it better. That's what it should be like for most women! And it is a wise man who learns this skill and seeks to become an artist at playing on his wife's heartstrings.

I wish for you such a virtuoso. These men are rare and, there's that drum again—they don't often come ready-built this way.

Which leads me to the second biological difference you must recognize:

2. *Most men need sex more often than women.*

No rules can be laid down which apply to every marriage.

Frequency of intercourse is something each couple must work out for themselves. Some couples in union may be happy with gratification once each week. Others would find this much too little sexual fare for their more vigorous appetites. There are certain marriages where sex is a beautiful part of every day's experience. Because each human being is different, it follows that each combination of human beings will vary. It is also likely that even the most thoroughly mated couples will differ from time to time and perhaps season to season. For this reason, to apply the same standards for every marriage would be sheer folly.

You do well to remember always that quality is more important than quantity in nearly everything you can mention. But from the marriages I have seen in consultation, it is apparent that *how often* usually matters most to the man and the *how to* is most important to the woman.

Yet, no matter the frequency, the main thing is to come to it joyfully. Learn to rest with it. The majority of wives who complain that it exhausts them will find their weariness in their head. Of course, there are variations in every rule and sometimes physical problems should be examined. There are even exceptions to the fact that most men like to think of themselves as sexual athletes. Some women complain that their husbands are never interested. This is not how it should be, and it needs looking into by the experts when it becomes a problem.

There may also be days when even the most vigorous man is so sapped of energy by his real or imaginary troubles that he is devoid of sexual desire. Don't become hysterical and don't take it personally if this happens now and then. You will learn to read him well and be wise enough to graciously decline sometimes for his sake. Perhaps he's done to exhaustion now and you'd do well to quiet your own interest. In marriage, it is best to measure emotions against the bigger background of time and effort and tender, loving care.

However, there will be no exceptions to this rule: You are a prudent wife when you look on sex, in part, as your opportunity to be a blessing to your husband. The tender women train themselves to receive a large measure of contentment just from contenting their men.

It is not true, in my counseling experience, that both parties to the union *need* the same results every time. I have read some writers who say that a man must be able to bring his wife to climax on every occasion of sexual love. In my judgment there is just one thing wrong with this supposition—it simply isn't so.

Some women tell me that they love to minister to their husband's emotional needs even when they care nothing at all about physical culmination for themselves.

I suspect that there are many marriages which could be considerably improved if both parties properly understood and accepted this. Some men have been falsely informed that they are failures if they cannot put their wives into ecstasy every time they reach that point themselves. This may be nothing short of selfishness on the man's part. He does wrong to set up goals which only meet some neurotic need of his own. How often he brings her to fruition should be *her* choice, not his. It takes a wise young husband to understand that his wife needs to be treated not as the passionate creature he dreamed about in teen fantasies, or read about in cheap sex books, or heard described with lurid words by the amateur in the locker room.

She needs to be treated as the woman she is! You can help him comprehend this if you can convince him that part of the time your only satisfaction-need is for him to be satisfied. In other words, you can have a mental enthusiasm for closeness even when your body is not enthusiastic in the same way as his.

But this must not continue forever. There are times when a husband is happier if his wife's exuberance matches his own. As we have said, it is usually true that man is the initial center of passion. Then sometimes she must become a center of passion on the occasions of her own choosing. At other times they become the center of passion together.

This is delicate doing and you must love it, work at it, and care enough to make it whatever is natural and good for the two of you.

A few paragraphs back we touched on a matter worth another look. You are wise to discuss together what you were taught about sex in your teens. Unfortunately, many parents even today have not presented this side of life to their children in a healthy way. Some boys picked up all they know about sex in the low places of other minds. Some girls grew up in a vacuum here. Others got their ideas by osmosis from a mother whose concept of women and sex was "this is our fate, this martyrdom!" It will help you both to know more about your own mental histories on this subject. Scared little girls and sex-obsessed boys don't come built that way in the first place. We are all partly what we picked up on the way, and this is another reason why gentleness is very much in order during the early seasons of nuptial love. It is also one more visible evidence that sex as a sacrament is the right basic concept.

There is one more thing to remember about wise wives and husbands whose sex drive seems unquenchable. The smart girls do not ration their men. They do not prescribe time, nor place, nor frequency, nor circumstances, nor manner. In my next letter I'll tell you more about these things, but right here let's run this by for a look:

I have known dozens of men who left home for sexual entertainment and many of them belonged to women who insisted on always dictating the terms!

There is one other death knell to sexual happiness which you should guard carefully. This is sounded whenever a woman thinks of sex as a prize to be awarded when he has been an especially good boy. Whenever she holds it out to him as a bribe, she contributes a number one prospect for the women who go for casual affairs.

The truth is that both "boughten sex" and "getting it on the side" are never completely satisfying. They couldn't be. If sex is holy and it needs the compassion of true concern to make it complete, then you will see this at once—substitutes are really not preferable to most men. But many males do settle for "seconds." Sometimes it is the woman they would love to love fully who has driven them to their revolt.

It's big, big business, isn't it? I hope you're not growing weary of the theme that marriage at its best is a lifework for two people at their best.

Mature partnership is an artistic achievement which doesn't come as a lucky row of beans on a bingo card. Sex may be one of nature's instincts, but it is not "natural" in the same sense as the casual, largely self-centered, and sometimes violent manner of the lower animals.

But men are like animals in this sense—they are much more ready on quick notice than the opposite of the species. Most young men come into marriage with a large reservoir of frustration which has accumulated through their growing years. This is one reason it is important for you to keep from having babics too soon. If enough time passes before that precious third party enters the scene, Vincent will make a better husband in the long run. Not only is it essential that you learn to adjust to each other before you both must adjust to number three—it is good for you both if you can thoroughly clear your system of the things you had to backlog before it was legal.

If a baby comes quickly, of course you will love the little darling and do your best with the circumstances at hand. But the child will have a better mother and father if they have spent plenty of time learning each other and pouring out their love to each other with no competition for the first few years.

You have always loved children, and you'll be a perfectly wonderful mother after the manner of your own. But, take it from me, your man needs sex and lots of it even when it may be the farthest thing from your mind. Convince him if you can that you love him so much you enjoy sharing your charms with him simply because he is in the mood for more.

Here is another beatitude for you. Let's call it, "Beatitude for an always-warm marriage": *Blessed is the woman who can celebrate her husband's virility with a true generosity that often seeks not so much to be loved as to love.*

Gratefully,
Dad

The Saint and the Sweet Little Sinner

My dear Karen,

Early in our marriage a wise clergyman friend of your mother gave her what he called his "description of the ideal wife." At first reading it may seem a bit risqué. But when you turn it around in your mind a few times you'll come to see that it is more good sense than impropriety.

The perfect mate for any man, said he, is: *"An angel in the home and a devil in bed!"*

Most men have an innate hope that their wife will be a combination of that old phrase, "The saint and the sweet little sinner!"

But the wives I have known who could qualify for such accolades are in the minority. I see their opposite often in consultation. Some of them proudly announce, "I never refused him!" They remind me of hopeful heroes waiting in line for the purple heart.

That might be the worst thing you could say about your marriage. Any man gets weary if he must always make the first move. Perhaps you'll join the hosts who chant, "But my man never gets weary!" Actually, however, his constant demand may be the very outgrowth of his weariness.

So, let's start with this, and I'll give you a few pointers on becoming the saintly little demon who can keep her man the kind of man she wants him to be.

1. *Be sexually aggressive some of the time.*

Do you remember when we played hide-and-seek? It was lots of fun for everyone. But to play the game right you had to take your turn as seeker now and then.

The same thing is true of sex, and there are some profound reasons behind this.

Never forget that Vincent wants to be wanted. The fact that sex is more of a surface matter to men does not eliminate the male depth-factor completely. You can count on this: Your husband longs to believe that he's wonderful enough for you to yearn sometimes for his sexual companionship.

It matters everything to a man if he has a home where he knows he is of inestimable value as a man. The world may deflate him, but he will be restored within his own walls. He may be wounded deeply out there in the marketplace, but at home there is a balm for him. Your husband can stand much more in the rough and tumble of a cut-throat world if you have convinced him that there is a waiting emotional center where he is vitally important.

You will study his ups and downs and learn to read well his soul's condition. The more he feels frustrated in his plans; the day he has been roughly handled by his superiors; when the big contract did not come through, or if in any way you sense that he has been put down somewhere—this is the time when you move in to indicate that your whole soul and body would welcome a closeness to him. Sex is a God-ordained means of assuring your partner that he is the most important person in the world right here, right now.

Actually, no matter how well things are going there is a measure of basic loneliness in every heart, male or female. I suspect that much of the moral laxity of our day is not alone immorality for immorality's sake. Some of it is a crying of the human soul for belonging. By sex, when it is right, we move out of our island existence to become a part of the mainland.

Glands are in need of release and sex is a biological clearance worth everything to the man who needs this cleansing. But it is much more than that. It is a confidence booster, a solace for injured pride, a psychological upward thrust when his soul cries out for a lift.

The surprise element is also a welcome feature to most men. Some night on your way home from somewhere, one day on a picnic just for the two of you, on the beach, in the woods, anywhere under the sun or the moon and stars where you are safe together—these are moments men cherish forever. This is a truth to build on. He will love you more with his soul if you overwhelm him now and then when he wasn't expecting your need for his body.

Learn to interpret him well and you be the seeker some of the time. Because most men think about sex more than women, the proper amount of aggression in you will add zest to his anticipation.

2. *Don't be afraid of experiment and variety.*

There is no need for me to write you a manual on sexual procedures. You have attended courses in marriage, and there are excellent books on this theme for those who need them.

The main thing I want to say here is that sex ought to be fun. It is not meant to be deadly serious all the time.

If you are to discover its fullest joys, you must come to this relationship as uninhibited as you can possibly be. You should give each other freedom to love in whatever way comes naturally to you both.

Some wives have never been told that the unusual may occur, and, when it does, this should be examined by both partners to the union as naturally as possible. Many women simply lack the knowledge that there are numerous positions and interesting variations.

So this is worth remembering: *There is nothing wrong with anything you may wish to do in your sex life provided it is pleasing to you both and not harmful to either.*

My heart goes out to the horror-stricken who come for counseling because of some "awful" suggestion their husband suddenly presented. They tell their story haltingly, and the word "perverted" is often included in their account. Perhaps somewhere in your girlhood you picked up ideas of perversion which have stayed with you. This term ordinarily makes reference to relations between members of one sex. When it refers to marriage, it means that one member of the union forces the other resulting in his or her psychological hurt.

You must teach yourself that nothing is perverted nor ugly nor unclean between you and Vincent if it is a new intimacy shared out of mutual desire for something novel, a fuller yearning for each other.

Some couples will be wise enough to know that certain unusual developments may be born out of neurotic needs which have never been satisfied. We have discussed the fact that many men carry with them into adulthood the infant's longing to be thoroughly related to the mother.

It is my experience in counseling that men who had a "weak" mother-son connection may be particularly fascinated by experimental sex. If hers was a "smother-love" or some other attempt to dominate; if he still clings emotionally to her in an unnatural way; or if he felt a maternal neglect and never really touched "home base" there; then there may be all kinds of unusual ideas in him which need working through. (Once again, you must realize that there are exceptions to every rule in these deep inner entanglements.) But you can best help him understand himself by talking it out together, by tenderness in inner research, and by a sex life which is complete in every way desirable to you both.

Remember the rule: Whatever increases the pleasure of sexual intimacy is right if it is mutually desired and if it leads to complete sexual gratification without harm.

You may be sure that you are not inventing something for the world. Everything imaginable here has been tried and tested. But if you keep an open mind and a joyful heart, you may discover some great new thrills for yourselves.

3. *Keep your body as alluring as God meant it to be.*

One afternoon at five I was calling on a church member when she suddenly stood up, turned toward the door and said, "Now, if you will excuse me, Dr. Shedd, John comes home in half an hour and I always spend the last thirty minutes before he arrives getting myself ready for him."

She did this quite naturally. Then when she realized that she had asked me to leave she blushed and was very embarrassed.

But not I! I inwardly rejoiced for women such as this. I commended her highly without reserve, and as I went down the walk I caught myself humming, "Ah, Sweet Mystery of Life!" As I drove along headed straight for home, I thought how much better our world would be if every woman spent the same thirty minutes in like manner. I should also add that this particular woman has five children of variant sizes and all of school age. Don't ask me how she has organized them for this ritual! I'm not a woman so I don't know. But I do know this, her husband is very much in love with her.

Some women grow "dutchy" the minute that ring is on their finger. They wear clothes about the house which would go better at a hard-times party. There is simply no excuse for some of the things I see on women. I have found housewives, during the day, wearing color combinations which remind me of our friend Harrison McGill's classic remark. As he viewed that perfectly awful rug some "generous" soul had donated to the choir room, he said in amazement, "There simply is no such color as that, is there?"

Vincent may say he will love you no matter how you look. He may not seem to mind if you get fat and out of shape. But then again—there was that early date when someone at the school dance didn't see him come in with you on his arm. So this inquisitive buddy tapped him on the shoulder and, pointing to you, he asked, "Who's the new babe with the cute build?" Your man will never forget that night.

You are a beautiful girl, and there isn't any reason why you can't keep him figure-proud of his wife for a long time. And if you remember the wedding vows, he promises to love you "for better, for worse, for richer, for poorer," but there is no mention of loving "through thick and thin."

Of course, it's harder after the babies come. But you're up

against the stiffest competition in the marketplace these days. It's all over the place. Don't forget that these sirens do have a drawing power which is something to reckon with. From what I've seen, the best way to deal with this is to make it look pale and lusterless compared to what waits with open arms at his own address. There is no road to any other female so attractive to a healthy husband as the road home to his wife if he can share with her, either silently or openly, his inmost feelings both high and low.

If you're doing your homework, you'll not need to worry either when you are out together and he turns his head to review some passing arrangement of molecules which smacks of sex appeal. You have done a good thing when you can get him to share with you what he likes and does not like in other women.

The fact that you are married to each other does not mean that you will now be blind to the attractive features of others. There may even be fleeting moments during the sex act itself when minds which love each other deeply will stray a bit. Happy is the marriage where each partner can clear thoughts which need to go.

Take care also to dress yourself in the loveliest things you can afford in preparation for your intimate moments together. I think I have told you about my fine old assistant pastor who looked on me more as a son than as his fellow worker. He never had a boy and he loved to "father" me. So he would advise me on almost everything, and this is another gem your mother and I hold dear: "Son," he said, "you've got to save money somewhere, but there are two places where you should not cut down ever. Never try to save on food nor women's lingerie!"

This is sage advice from a salty saint who had a successful fifty years of love to back up his statement. Among your husband's most precious memories when he is not in your presence are these recollections of beauty shared when you were together.

The female of our species was created with seductive powers which have been debauched by sinners and maligned by moralists through the years. But do you suppose the world simply hasn't grown up to this truth—maybe women were made that way because that's how they are needed at the right time and in the right place?

History makes it plain that every civilization which has lost respect for marital fidelity has been relegated to the dump heap of material no longer useable for eternal construction.

The best protection I know against loose sex is a wife who knows the glories of womanhood and uses her natural charms to the maximum.

With high hopes for heavenly rapture,
Dad

Those Great Big Beautiful Dollars

My dear Karen,

In our married days at the seminary we went often to the warehouses on grocer's row. There was one place where they stacked cans of food clear up to the ceiling. It was like standing before a mountain of tin. There were big cans, little cans of every size, shape, and condition.

There was, however, this one difference between the cans here and those you see on your grocer's shelves. *These had no labels.* Because of this slight omission they were for sale at three cents per can. The sorters had tossed them aside as "damaged," which meant anything from a major dent to some minor flaw which could only be noted by the inspector's eye.

The man who ran the warehouse guaranteed this one thing—there was food of some variety in each can. He also claimed that nothing was spoiled, but, as he said, "For three cents what you gonna lose? You pay your money and take your choice."

Do you know how to tell the difference between peaches and plums by the shake of a can? Could you, by ear, distinguish carrots from corn? Well, your mother and I became well-nigh infallible as shakers of edibles.

Of course, no one is perfect; so, we sometimes drew chili for dessert. It sounds like fruit cocktail! Thank goodness, we had an icebox and plastic covers were cheap; so, we lived it up and laughed and ate away. In fact, it was great fun and we looked forward to our semi-monthly outing to the can hills.

For three dollars on payday we could purchase one hundred cans of nourishment, and the man was right—it was all palatable and all good! Sure, there were times when we wished we might be free of this small-change living and shop at the stores with the nice folks. But as we look back on it now, we list those days with our happiest memories.

The Bible says, "It is good for a man that he should bear the yoke in his youth." It also is good for a woman. And it is just about the finest for a man and a woman together if they are faced with the necessity of living largely on love for the first few years.

More important than the house you live in is what kind of you is living in the house!

How much the divan cost matters less than what you share there in visiting and dreaming and *inamorata!*

Your greatest need right now is not for a new stove, nor for new pots and pans, but for new fires to refine you and warm you and make your heart glow. Though it may be hard to believe, you are fortunate indeed that your budget is limited.

Speaking of budgets, one of my favorite quotes on same is this from an unknown oracle, "A budget, strictly enforced, is like long underwear. If you need it, you better have it. If you don't, it scratches!"

You will probably learn that the man is right. You'll no doubt find it essential, and there will be times when it doesn't wear well. But here are some secrets to budgeting money which we have found invaluable.

Let's begin with the first things first. At our house, as you know, we have lived by this money-motto:

"Give ten percent, save ten percent, and spend the rest with thanksgiving and praise!"

We've never regretted that day when we made this decision. Some precepts, adopted early, make a mighty difference in the years to come.

That ten percent giving commitment is no place for faint hearts. When your first check comes in, you'll sit down and count up the bills, and you'll be tempted to join the "our-problem-is-different-from-everybody-else's" brigade.

You may rationalize. "When we get more, *then* we'll give more!" But you won't. This is one of those things where you either do or you don't.

It's your life to live, but you asked me to point you toward heaven on earth and, dollar-wise, this is "Gate One" to some wonderful discoveries.

Many people I see these days are desperately afraid. Some of these shivering souls are frightened by many things. But one of their major anxieties is that the good will be gone before they get their share.

It is true that some are clinging to fearsome memories out of their yesterdays. We must make allowance for their neuroses. But many couples would be richly blessed by a new philosophy of giving. They need to know that it is not enough to have "goods." These things are fleeting, but the secret to "the good life" is not in possessing more things.

The decision to give that ten percent first may also be your safety factor when the day of your prospering comes. You can't imagine it now, but the time will arrive when your money-pressures begin to let up. As this happens, some people start making their own rules. But if you have adopted certain basic principles in your lean years, you'll find that they act as safeguards when the fruits of your labor begin to ripen.

So, this is number one—Give ten percent and give it first!

Saving that second ten percent will also call for strict discipline. There are several reasons, however, why it is worth what it costs.

For one thing, it can prevent some of the foolish mistakes of overspending which we'll consider in our next letter.

Then, too, a mutually agreed savings program will give you the solid satisfaction of knowing that you are insuring your future. The stormy days will not catch you unprepared, nor will your son's education, nor that trip you need to broaden your horizons, nor even the wedding for your lovely daughter.

Operating on a definite principle can also free your mind to concentrate more clearly for better performance at your work. The time which you might waste in worry can now be dedicated to added efficiency which will guarantee an even more substantial base to your future.

Another merit which comes from saving a set percentage is that it might protect you against the dangers of oversaving. We see these poor souls too in the counseling room. They are victims of the poverty complex which compels them to hang on too tight to too much.

These folks assume that when they have more they'll be liberated to enjoy their accumulation. But they probably won't. Sometimes you can read it in their eyes—true joy is not to be found in stocks and bonds and bigger bank accounts. They are not sad because of their losses. Theirs is a money-melancholy which only increases as their gains increase.

It is a pitiful truth that *having* more sometimes leads to *being had!*

Let's close this one down with an observation on a familiar saying. It is often misquoted—"Money is the root of all evil!" But that is not how the original reads. Instead, it says "The *love of money*" is the origin of the error.

So now and then move your eyes from concentration on the

intakes and check to see if your *outlets* are in good order. The fact is that what goes from your pocket has a direct bearing on what comes in. This is a law of life.

In his original creation the Heavenly Father included certain of these unfailing principles. Out of his love he provided for the needs of all his children and he built his universe to meet these needs. When you observe his rules and live by them, he can tax the remotest sources to meet your every requirement.

I hope you will early learn this truth: If you keep your part of the covenant, you can never, ever outgive God!

Keep looking up,
Dad

Want Your Own Wants

My dear Karen,

"*Make the very most of all you've got and make the very least of what you can't get yet!*"

This little jewel came from Grandma Davidson. I called her "the sage of Sugar Creek," which was my first student pastorate. Grandma had twenty-seven children and grandchildren. For Sunday dinner, it was some sight to sit with them at her table which originated in the dining room and extended to the far wall of her parlor.

Your mother and I were engaged, so I had my antenna out for guidance. While we leveled a mountain of fried chicken and asked for seconds on her homemade ice cream, my inner buzzers were getting the signal. These happy couples had what we wanted. They were very much alive to each other and at peace with their world.

I often stayed at Grandma's on my weekend visits. So one day I asked her to teach me what she taught her own "younguns," as she called them. Since she knew that her pastor friend was about to "be hitched" (quoting her again), she did what her Bible said—"She opened her mouth with wisdom."

Out of her numerous suggestions, I pass on to you here this brief item which I heard her say over and over—"Make the very most of all you've got and make the very least of what you can't get yet!"

It was clear that these solid unions of her sons and daughters were no accident. They had taken her words to heart, and one mark of their love was a rare quality which many couples miss. They had learned to enjoy their enjoyments and to deny their denials.

There are two facts which might apply to "loving that man" as we loiter a bit before this gem from Grandma Davidson's collection. One of these is particularly for feminine ears. The other may be something you and Vincent can use together.

1. *Give praise to your man and glory to God with loud "Thanks" and "Nice going" and "Hurrahs for you!"*

We've been at this door before in our letters. Whenever I seem to be taking you repeatedly down some well-beaten path you can be sure it's for one reason only. I've seen this so often that it bears repetition. In my work as a counselor I have come on too many women who believe they can "drive" their husbands to success with stern commands or subtle innuendoes.

We both know that some men are laggards and their laziness has an adverse effect on the whole family. But those are not our consideration here. I'm thinking rather of the host of earnest workers who are giving it their best and still can't satisfy that demanding woman at home.

Here are some statements from such ill-favored husbands to illustrate my point. The first is out of my own experience.

One day in my study I heard a worn-out husband make this tragic admission: "I've had it. It's an awful thing to say but I've got to say it. She's all right in her place, but her place hasn't been dug yet! I'm so desperate I'm even willing to give up the kids to get away from her pounding!"

The second comes from my reading. Heine, the German poet, is reported to have said that should he die before his wife he certainly hoped she would remarry in order that there might be one person in the world to regret his passing!

Read the first quote again and weep! Read the second once more and smile! But never, never allow yourself to employ that sinister smile which some women use to berate their husband's livelihood.

If you must make some changes, then do it intelligently together by honest discussion in love. Mix your phrases with praises for his best efforts and let him know your every word is for boosting him up and not for blowing him down.

Thanksgiving and gratitude are absolute musts for another reason which you may not have considered. Now and then a horrible thought skitters across nearly every male mind. If he is married and if he works, *he may feel trapped* when he's not up to his best. He once was free but now he must labor for his wife, for his children, and for those myriad spongy things at home which soak up his hard-earned dollars. When this is at its worst, he may even see his woman as a particular type of parasite. There she sits reading an interesting book, watching a soap opera, drinking coffee with the girls, while he slaves at the salt mines to make all this possible.

Fortunately, these are only flashes and, in part, this is somewhat impersonal. When he comes back to center he probably wouldn't even consider trading marriage to you for life on the loose again.

We have talked about warm words and warm gratitude and a warm body as an antidote for all this. There is still another mitigator you might keep in mind. *Let him have a healthy amount of say in how the money should be spent!*

There may be certain checks he likes to write. Or maybe he'll wish to handle them all. Unless he's a ruinous financier (some men are), he may prefer to preside over the funds while you admire over his shoulder. Especially during your early years, this "chancellor of the exchequer" role may be what his ego needs. If you laud him and boost his opinion of himself sufficiently, he may come home one day, as your father did, and say, "Honey, will you take over running the budget? I have so many important things to do!"

2. *Want your own wants!*

Some mathematical wizard has figured that the average modern family is exposed to another sales pitch 1,158 times daily. I don't know where nor how he gets his figures. But you know, when you stop to consider it, that all the adjectives of our language are harnessed to race the chariots of commerce and trade.

Turn on the radio, read the newspapers, flick on your television, read a magazine. Everywhere the swamis cry, "Lo, here! Lo, there! ... Buy these! Buy them! Hurry, now, don't miss these bargains.... Be the first in your crowd to own one! Everybody who is anybody serves our brand.... You want to 'come up'? Then smoke our smokes.... Mother, father, sister, brother, you'll all smell well with our deodorant! ... Go this very minute to the cut-rate store! Pay your money for a bottle of these! ... They're just right for what hurts you!" and, if nothing hurts, they're right for that, too!

The sharpies will get you if you don't watch out! They have a way of stealing the joy right out from under you. Their stuff is like dope. It's easy to get on but hard to get off. They'll try to convince you that what you make yourself can't possibly be as good as what they have made for you. With all the gusto of the old-time evangelist, they'll call you to glue your eyes on the new drapes, the new car, the new rug, or some other new item with an appalling appeal.

They'll even lend you the money to buy it and they make it so simple!—"Get your loan by mail!" And if you *have* fallen into the seller's traps there are other barkers to cry, "Now, wouldn't you like to consolidate your debts?"

When your mother and I were in school we borrowed from one of these "pay only us" places! I suppose it was not so, but it seemed that every month when we made our payments we owed a little bit more than the month before!

Be wary of borrowing at all, but, if you must, do it where the good guys are. If you aren't careful about this you may have innocently exchanged a few errors for a whole bunch. An anonymous poet puts it better than I could when he says:

> If a bank won't make the loan,
> Go without until they do.
> If it isn't good for them,
> It can't be good for you!

I see them often, these foolish people, who have clamored so greedily for "stuff" that they have overextended in their hysteria. Then, in their panic, they grasp for more and clutch so tightly to "things" that life's true values slip from their hands.

So, want your own wants! Don't let the "Buy, Buy, Buy" boys pilfer the pleasure of your present enjoyments! Make the very most of all you've got and make the very least of what you can't get yet!

Yea, yea and nay, nay!
Dad

Happy Housekeeping

My dear Karen,

An old English proverb makes this claim: "There is but one hour a day between a good housewife and a bad one!"

Since my lifework is not housekeeping, I couldn't possibly have much to say of significance here.

But I do get into many homes, and I have observed some things which I offer humbly, realizing I am way over my head in this field.

1. The good housewives I see seem to be organized.

We teach the custodians at the church that they should clean these rooms Monday, that section on Tuesday, and especially make sure to tidy up the sanctuary on Saturday in preparation for Sunday's service. Maybe this English proverb carries its punch in the fact that it smacks heavy of system.

2. The good housewives I see take pride in their homes.

There are two extremes here and "right" must be somewhere in the middle. Some women make wrecks of themselves keeping a three-room apartment. It is not true that all female ulcers come from the big houses. As we've said before, most men grow weary of women who fuss and fume too much over details. I've seen some otherwise good marriages destroyed by perfectionist wives.

The opposite of this "a place for everything and everything in its place" female is no better. I was in a home the other day where we had to move great stacks of clothes to be ironed, magazines, ball gloves, brassieres, skates, and even a parakeet cage from chairs and divan before either one of us could sit down. Being a country boy, I also observed that they might have planted corn in the corners. The dirt was that thick.

With some things the blend is the thing, and I suspect that housekeeping is one of these. A sense of pride—but not too much! The casual life—but not too casual!

3. *The good housewives I see have somehow learned to make fun out of duty.*

Perhaps "pleasure" would be a better word than fun. Most men have no idea how much there is to housekeeping. They find out, of course, when something happens to mama for a time. It never occurs to most of us males that there are floors to wax, pans to clean, sheets to change, furniture to polish, diapers to wash, blouses to iron, towels to fold, and so on *seriatim* and in *extenso.*

I, for one, am simply overjoyed that God made me a man. But some women seem to love it, they take pleasure in it, they make fun out of it.

As I was telling you, this is not my field and I better get out of it this very minute. But before I do here is another favorite proverb of mine. I keep this one also under the glass on my desk top.

"*Most footprints on the sands of time were made with work shoes!*"

Happy housekeeping,
Dad

A Savory Smell from the Kitchen

My dear Karen,

My commentary on cooking must have help from somewhere. You know I speak the truth. In the area of the oven and range my amateur standing has never been questioned.

Whenever your mother went to the hospital for bearing the latter members of our family offspring, I gave it my best. But my best was sadly lacking, and I can still hear the chorus-united, "Daddy, please, can't we go out for hamburgers tonight? *Please?*"

So, since we have under our roof one who "don't know from nothin'" (quoting your elder brother) and a true queen of the culinary arts, I asked the latter to give us a hand.

Then one day she presented me with what I think is a very nice thing. Here is your mother's alphabet for savory smells and meals at their best. In a few spots I've added a parenthesis.

"A" is for attractive service! Be alert to the beautiful colors in foods. Yellows and greens and red and browns put carefully together can make your meals a thing of beauty.

"B" is for blessings at the meal! Notice I said *at* the meal! When your father was a boy he said that nobody dared take one bite until they had all "said grace" together. You know that many a piping-hot dish could be spoiled under this rigorous rule. So, we've always thanked God during our meals or afterward. We like it this way, and I have a feeling the Lord must like it too at our house!

"C" is to cook according to your budget! We learned in our married days at school that there are numberless ways to fix macaroni. Shopping can be a sporty game if you study the ads, spot the specials, and watch for the weekend bargains. You can do all this and still buy quality foods.

"D" stands for don't let him make his own breakfast! Especially for brides and mothers with children, it's "early to rise" for keeping your man in a mellow mood.

"E" is to eat by candlelight now and then! You know how happy the Brocks are. They tell us this is a regular event with them. Jim

puts on his suit and tie. Joann dresses in a lovely gown, and they sit by the fireplace with soft music, candles, and the children farmed out. They say it's one of the highlights at their house.

"F" is for festive occasions! We make the twenty-ninth of each month our "special" day because we were married that day in May. I know you'll remember our gala holiday dinners. I can hardly wait for the next one!

"G" is to go out together now and then! You will think that down in the future there will be plenty of time to live relaxed. This is a mirage. Tomorrow you will be busy, too. So budget some of your money for good times with each other alone.

"H" is to have your meals ready on time! Gadding about is part of the fun of being a woman. But never, never, never be about your gadding when you should be about getting your meals.

"I" is for imagination, a gift of the Lord. This is particularly good for what a famous eastern preacher refers to in his sermon, "Putting the Lure into the Leftovers."

"J" stands for joyful thoughts! In my home economics major we learned that digestion and attitudes are closely related. One of our psychiatrist friends points to "I'm fed up!" "You don't expect me to swallow that!" and "I can't stomach him!" to prove his claim that ulcers may come more from moods than from foods.

"K" is to kiss before the meal! You know one man who does this even in public. If there is one moment when I feel like a queen with the court looking on, this is the moment. And it also gives me a special little flutter at home.

"L" is for lingering when the meal is over! One time when your dad had taken you on an overnight trip to some speaking engagement, he came back with a lesson he's never forgotten. I guess you were ten or eleven and this is what he said, "For miles and miles we saw signs about 'The World's Deepest Well' in a small Kansas town. But when we came to it we simply couldn't stop if I was to make the banquet on time. Karen was quiet for some distance and then she said, 'Daddy, I feel sorry for you! You hurry so fast you miss the fun things!'" Right there he made the decision to slow down, and you did us all a big favor with that one.

"M" is for manners! "Thank you" and "No, thank you," "Please" and "Pardon me" make the meal nicer for everyone. This is in your domain and I'd see that the whole family knows, "This is not Sloppy-Joe's!"

"N" stands for nourishing foods! Have well-balanced meals for good health's sake!

"O" is to often prepare his favorite dishes! Learn how he likes them and serve them enough.

"P" is to plan ahead! It saves time and energy and fussing and fretting and headaches and money!

"Q" is for 'quainting yourself with the cookbooks! Learn to thank God there are people who know more than you do.

"R" is to remember the little things! Napkins and all the utensils, salt and pepper at both ends of the table, relishes, and flowers in a pretty vase are nice for some situations. (Never for ours. They get knocked over every time!)

"S" is for sharing with others! Let him bring his friends home. The children will also love you if they can invite theirs. Of course, you must train him and them to phone when delayed and let you know in advance. One of my friends thought she would "cure" her thoughtless husband forever when she heard by the grapevine that his boss was in town. She knew this was the night it would happen. So she threw on the bread and bologna, tossed on luncheon meat and lettuce, added tomatoes, mustard, and pickles. Guess what happened? The "visiting fireman" said it was the best meal he'd had in a week!

"T" is for television—turn it off! This goes also for radio and the news. (You know it requires a unanimous vote of our family to watch TV while we eat. There was one awful day which Peter and I will never forget. The Lions and Bears were playing their championship game. Someone voted "No!" I can't remember the culprit. This is another nice thing the Lord does for his children. As time passes, he dims our remembrance of who did what to whom.)

"U" stands for unexpected surprises! Someone describes one of the saints of yesterday with this charming line, "She always kept open for everyone the soul's east window of divine surprise." An extra-special menu which will tickle his taste buds, a classy dessert, or the exciting new recipe from one of our friends can work wonders.

"V" is for variety! We've said this several times, but it's easy to get in a rut. Experimenting is fun, so diversify for the good of all.

"W" is to welcome him warmly! This goes for when he comes home, when he comes to the table, when he comes with a problem, when he comes for love.

"X" stands for 'xtra helpings! Some need them. Some don't. Yet nobody likes stinginess. (A cute poem comes to mind. It's more about 'xtra pounds than 'xtra helpings, but I think you'll like it:

"My girlfriend's waist is 42.
She eats her meals in haste.
And so, you see it's really true....
Haste make waist!")

"Y" is for your own appearance! Grooming and cleanliness and fixing your pretty face to its very best are worth your attention.

"Z" is for zest! One of my good friends is fond of saying, "A warm meal can be ruined by a cold-hearted cook!" Learn to enjoy your kitchen and fill it with love from your soul!

So, love that man and love him well from behind your stove. On a recent trip through the south we stopped at a little café in Kentucky. Above the door was a sign which read, "Something superior for your interior!" That's a fine goal for a housewife, too, isn't it?

Best wishes for a savory marriage,
Dad

If Adversity Strikes

My dear Karen,

The other day I was in a home where some well-wisher had done an attractive piece of needlepoint. It hung in an antique frame and the words of the woven motto were: "May there be just enough clouds in your sky to make a beautiful sunset!"

Very nice thought there, don't you think? But the reason I had come to this particular house was that the clouds were coming down now. The beautiful sunset had scattered, destruction was threatening, and the sky was getting darker all the time. There was bitterness and raging and life was rough, very rough!

The stern facts stood out bolder than the lovely thoughts in needlepoint. As I looked up there once more, I felt like stepping across the room to turn the motto to the wall. But I stayed where I was. We were hoping that the sun would return. Then the words would have meaning again and the sentiment would go nicely once more. Yet right now these hearts were moaning and their souls were bending low.

You know that like most parents we wish for you and Vincent a pleasant, peaceful life. The unknown poet puts well our prayer in his quaint line, "May the song of the dove be heard in your love and the small fowls make melody."

Yet, life is not always what we might prefer. Trouble in some form is a part of living for most people. There are a few who appear to have an inside track with the gods of good fortune. But for ordinary citizens there will be troubles and sickness, losses and woe, death and dilemma.

So what can you do if life gets hard? There are some things worth remembering. Suppose we call them "The A-B-C's for Adversity!"

A. One answer for these times is to *calmly face the fact that you will not be exempt from the harsh and troublesome.*

I would not purposely make you morbid, but you should know this: I see many foolish couples who go blindly along under the false assumption that a love such as theirs will be excused from bad luck and stormy weather. They mistakenly think that their license to marry included some guarantees for a life of ease.

You have taken a mature attitude toward all this when you say in unison: *"We seek a happy marriage with wholeness of heart, but we do not expect to reach the promised land without going through some wilderness together."*

B. A second help for the hard times is this natural follow-up of number one—*God does not promise his followers freedom from trouble.*

He only pledges that he will be with us when the thunder claps and the lightning flashes. I am glad you have learned the value of a vital religious faith.

We'll talk about this at length before we are done, but many people need nothing more than they need a new understanding of living continually with the Lord no matter what comes. Their idea of "being religious" is to attend church on Sunday. When they leave their places of worship, it is rather like giving God a wave of the hand and saying, "See you next week! Same time! Same place!"

One of my psychiatrist friends recently sent a troubled man to see me. When he called to make an appointment for his client he made this interesting statement, "I think we've cleared up most of his mental problems. He's a churchgoer and I think you might help him. What he needs now is someone who can help him find his answer eighteen inches lower down. He has it in his head. Now he needs it in his heart."

Praises be, this is not your problem. The wick of your lamp runs deep into the oil of the Eternal. You've been friends with the Lord for a long time and you know how to pray. You have learned that trouble does not mean God has gone off and left you. It does mean that he can use this for bringing you to higher ground if you will let him.

C. A third strengthening factor looms large as I go back over the case histories of marriages I have seen from the inside. This is that you do a big thing when you *determine together that the hard things will be used as sealers rather than dividers of your union.*

Perhaps we can illustrate this by an amusing tale I heard from a rough old sheepherder friend of our Colorado days. He said that when a pack of fierce dogs plunder, or the coyotes come, there is one all-important difference between wild horses and wild asses. According to his account, when these deadly foes attack, the wild horses put their heads together in a tight center, tails to the windward side, and *proceed to kick the devil out of their adversaries.* But, if we can believe his reporting, when the wild asses are put upon, they place their heads toward the enemy, their tails to the inside, and *they kick the devil out of each other.*

I don't know whether he was "pulling my leg" as he loved to do. Yet his story does pack a wallop, doesn't it?

Particularly, I think it is a message for the married. I am sorry to report that most of the couples who come to my study remind me of the wild asses. They come kicking at each other, or at themselves, or at their marriage.

This is too bad. These husbands and wives have not learned their A-B-C's for handling adversity.

So, this is a good credo for a victorious union: "Why life is like this we do not know! But we know this! What happens is not so important as what we do with what happens. One day the sun will return and we will be better, finer people. God is never far away! Nothing shall separate us from togetherness with each other and with him."

Take courage,
Dad

Sometimes Look Outward

My dear Karen,

True love of the highest kind is not gazing starry-eyed forever into each other's optics. In our last letter we talked about facing inward at the right time in the right way. But looking fondly toward each other is not the sole purpose of marriage.

So let's talk about keeping the windows of your home clear for an outward look. I recently heard a psychiatrist friend present an interesting paper on mental health. He said one thing which bears repeating. He told us that he advised one of his patients, "You should cut some windows in your selfishness. Notice the neighbor working his garden. Watch folks passing along the street. Count the cars as they go by. This will be excellent therapy. You have forgotten that there are other people in the world besides yourself."

This physician of the mind touches here on one of the counselor's major problems. Some couples, as we have said, look too little at their mates. The major requirement of others is a look inside themselves. Then, as the doctor says, there are those whose curative depends on looking outward together.

Here are some places where this applies.

Let's begin with "*friends.*"

It is good for you and Vincent to be "best friends." Yet I have observed some marital friendships of the "me and thee" variety which started as a cozy little exclusiveness and never advanced beyond that. I hope you will learn to snuggle down into your environment. But don't let your environment snuggle down around you so much that you never share your warmth with friends.

Some of these selfish houses with the barred door eventually become little more than nursing homes for a mutual narcissism.

So make friends and share your love because that's one of the big reasons why it was given you. Selfishness in any form is sin, and unless you work out the love which God has worked in, you may be a part of the world's evil rather than its blessing.

That you will choose your friends well we know by your history. In marriage certain friendships broaden insights; others are for laughs; and then there are those whose companionship is like a tree where you find shade.

There are also dangerous friendships which will gradually drain your sense of holiness unless you are alert to their fade-away influence. These are frequently in the "everybody-does-it" crowd. They are the "group-think" people who may drag you down into the moral sag of the times if you let them. With the gang where "everything goes," everything may be gone before someone has the courage to stand up and be different.

You never were a prig, and I'm sure you won't be two prigs strutting your piety together. But there is a vast difference between prudishness and true goodness born of inner conviction. Sometimes one couple's fortitude may be a blessing to others who only needed a leader. For some situations the sole solution is a clear "goodbye!" Whether you stand alone or turn up companions who were waiting for someone else to take the initiative is not important. What does matter is for you to continually remind yourselves that *you are here to transform the world and not to let the world transform you.*

Another outward move which needs consideration is the turn toward *relatives and in-laws.*

May your relationships with "the relations" be increasingly

pleasant as the years pass. But some go in the opposite direction. Many people knock on the counsel room door for help with this.

Some of these originate when a husband or wife insists on perpetually burning incense to "dear old mom" or "good old dad." Others are nourishing bitter hatreds which can be easily understood considering the treatment they received.

I would wish that the fates might excuse you from this problem. But if they do not there is one sure thing to remember. Whenever you are tempted to put your own or your husband's kinfolk in their place, remind yourself again—with some folks it's what you don't say that counts!

Whatever the feeling, it is good to turn now and then toward the homes from which you came. If these relationships are strained they usually are only more strained by staying away. "It's over the fields and through the woods to grandfather's house we go" may be a sentimental relic from the past. But you better believe this: You'll never have peace all the way to the center of your soul until you have worked out some kind of peace with brothers-in-law, sisters-in-law, parents-in-law, aunts, uncles, nephews, nieces, and the whole tribe. This *can* be accomplished, even if the only peace in this relationship is the peace in your own soul.

One more important outward swing of your doors bears the label, *social service.*

There is no community to which you could move, no open country where you might build your house, but that you have come into the zones of the unfortunate.

Some couples accept the pinched faces of the starved and forsaken as part of the scenery. Others look aghast and feel bad. Then they turn away to content themselves with feeling good because they felt bad.

Certain "vocal patriots" become armchair critics. Their chief targets are usually "the government" or "those folks" who are at least trying. This kind will propound their "wisdom (?)" as long as you listen. But their words are often only a substitute for action.

There are even mistaken saints who go to their prayer chambers to intercede on behalf of life's ill-favored. This is good, unless you make this your single contribution. God never accepts us on our knees if we should be standing up to some evil or moving out of our doors to blaze highways, cut channels, clear paths, and do what we can to extend the arm of mercy where it needs extension.

If you do adopt some worthy project as your challenge, you are in for discouragement. Often you will feel like crying, "What is *our* little effort against such odds?" Yet, if you give it a try and make an effort, you will discover another wellspring of satisfaction. This is the satisfaction which comes only to those who are dissatisfied enough to take up a post somewhere in the war against poverty, disease, and desolation.

William Allen White is purported to have said, "My advice to the garden clubs of our land is to raise more hell and fewer dahlias." Some of the advance guard of the human race have been "hell-raisers" for "heaven's sake."

Perhaps you will be moved to join a "community cause." Or you may feel an inner compulsion to declare yourself against some gaping wrong which you see clearly as an insult to society. Now your comfort and safety-first must give way to speaking out, even if you are misunderstood. Great things have been started by solo voices when there was no other voice to join them.

It is important that you check now and then to be sure you are not swept up in "good causes" to the neglect of some basic assignments with a prior claim. You will like this story of the weary husband who brought his wife down to earth one night with a thud.

She arrived home late from her political rally, plopped herself in the big chair, kicked off her shoes, and announced, "It was great, Henry! We're going to sweep the state!" Poor Henry who had done the dishes, put the children in bed, and struggled with the vacuum cleaner, listened her through. Then he came with this caustic comment, "Sounds great! Why don't you start with the living room?"

The tricky business of doing right for wrong reasons also needs checking now and then. Some reformers are merely blowing a neurotic foghorn out of a crack in their emotional structure. This is not good. The world needs only the clearest trumpets for social righteousness. The "slightly sick" doers of good may accomplish some things worthwhile, but they might also undermine what the healthy are building.

Sometimes in the church we see these "brothers and sisters of good causes" running about, mopping feverish brows, convinced that fate has assigned them to attend single-handed to the salvation of all. One mark of mental well-being in social service is to remember that you are not expected to clean up the whole earth.

You get the message. There are two common maladies here. One is the sickness of crusading in places meant for other reformers. The second is to close our doors to the trumpet sounds which *were* meant for our ears.

The growing "let's-don't-get-involved" philosophy is not for people with your abilities. "Under the Spreading Apathy" is more than a clever title for a book. This is a real threat to the nation. When too many nice folks become indifferent, the next step is likely to be indifference to the indifference, and this may be a sign that the end is approaching. Always one telltale mark of decay is the assumption that we are good merely because we have refrained from being bad.

So, if yours is a healthy marriage, you will be looking out, moving out, crying out some of the time. But, for goodness' sake, be constantly checking your motives.

The main motive, of course, is traceable to your very reason for living. In another letter we'll give further thought to the fact that you were not put here on earth, nor put into each other's arms, to serve only yourselves.

It is a startling realization when any couple faces this truth: *There is something more important in the world than our own happiness!*

I hope you will know the thrill which comes to those who leave the place better than they found it.

Think big,
Dad

When Nothing Works

My dear Karen!

Not for a moment would I attempt to convince you that all good wives have good husbands. It simply is not so.

Generally, it is true that you get what you pay for. But some souls pay the full price and receive no recompense. There are men who turn out to be bad matches for even the finest women. She may give him her all; he takes everything and gives her nothing.

There is no more desolate sight than a broken-hearted woman who put her whole soul into her marriage and got back only a heart full of broken dreams.

They say that life is ten percent what you make it and ninety percent how you take it. That is a very clever statement but, like many such, it doesn't cover the entire radius. I have seen some of the Lord's ladies who went ninety percent of the way, or even ninety-nine, and their reward was an absolute blank.

Of course, all this really has nothing to do with you and Vincent. We *know* your marriage will be a resounding success.

Yet, I did want to write this one letter to ask you to reserve a very special kindness for those who are not so fortunate. They need the tenderest touch your hand can give. They need a ready ear and a sincere friend to share their tears. So whenever this happens in the vicinity of your heart, make haste to open your soul with godly sympathy. You will also want to open your lips in a prayer for a better tomorrow than their shattered yesterdays have been.

The happier you are the more you must stretch out room inside yourself for those who have not found life so good and beautiful as you have found it.

Ten little letters make up a great word:

"Compassion!"

Yours for a compassionate heart,
Dad

Greater Than the Two of You

My dear Karen,

"I worship you!"—"You're an angel!"—"Our love is heavenly!"—these are welcome sounds to lovers' ears.

But be sure you understand them in their proper context.

Self-reverence may be good, and two selves in reverence for each other might be even better. But this might also be sick, very sick, unless this reverence is part of a larger reverence.

You will remember from your science courses that it is the sun which keeps the solar system from flying apart. The world and everything in it, including you and Vincent, would come undone if it were not for this magnetic force holding things together.

This is how it is with marriage. Two may be born in opposite hemispheres, or they may have grown up in the same block, but what matters most is this—*are they being held together at the center by a holy love which is stronger than their own?*

This is the basic question because of one inescapable fact. Even the most "divine" creature on earth has one thing in common with the rest of the populace—we are all human!

At our present stage of development, one bit of standard equipment on Homo sapiens is an innate tendency to selfishness.

Whether it was the amoeba in the swamp or the first creature on legs or the ape swinging from his tree or some shaggy-haired ancestor with club in hand, or whoever is to blame—the truth is that most of us have not evolved far enough to be free of this instinct to self-preservation.

"Look out for a number one!"—"I want what I want when I want it!"—"Me first, me second, me third!"—these are villains waiting in the wings of any marriage when the lover's song has died away.

You may determine that you *will* think of the other fellow first. You *will* try to see life through his eyes. You *will* be sweet and gentle and kind this whole day long. But, if you are like your dad, within thirty minutes this noble vow is one more beautiful theory murdered by a gang of brutal facts.

So where do we go from this dilemma?

The answer, as I have learned it at our house and observed it times without number in counseling with others, is the theme of this letter.

Here is *the key of keys* to love at its radiant best: *That couple who understands that their union is for Someone greater than the two of them has discovered the secret gate to marriage at its best.*

Let's take a look now at how you can bring your lives together to this blessed estate.

Recently, I heard some mathematically minded minister on the radio make these interesting claims. He cited the fact that one marriage in four ends in divorce. He said that for families who attend church regularly, the rate of broken homes is one in fifty-four. He further stated that for families who pray together, the ratio is one to five hundred.

He didn't say where he got his figures, but after hearing his testimony I made an analysis of my own experience.

My record looks like this. In twenty years I estimate that I have counseled with more than two thousand couples who came to me with their problems. This includes husbands, wives, or both of them together. Their problems ranged from triviality to tumult.

Now hear this! *I have never had one couple or one member of a marriage come to me with their troubles if they prayed together.* (There were a few, perhaps a dozen, who said, "We used to!")

So, this is my witness. One out of so many visits the clinics. One of this many is severed in the courts. But in my own experience, *one out of none* was broken beyond repair if they had slipped their joined hands into the hand of God through prayer.

Let me list for you here the prayer steps which I have recommended to hundreds of couples:

1. Make a compact that you will set aside some time each day when you look Godward together.

2. Select some devotional guide which suits you. There are many of these in the bookstores, and most churches have them on their literature racks.

3. When your appointed time has come, you sit together quietly while one of you reads the day's selection.

4. Now you talk over what you would like to pray about. If Vincent is concerned with something in his business, he may appreciate an opportunity to tell you this. Perhaps you will confess that he hurt your feelings this morning and you haven't been able to put that where it belongs. You may ask for clarification, if you need it, but you will not argue. You simple place before each other things which are on your hearts.

5. Then you hold hands, bow your heads, and pray silently to God as you understand him. It will probably be best if you do not begin by praying out loud together. Unless you have done this frequently, it may be so awkward and embarrassing that you won't keep it up after the first few attempts.

6. When you feel that you have "gotten through," you pray the Lord's Prayer together.

As you develop this art between you there will be times when your prayer will major in silent listening. Gradually, your perception enlarges until you understand that prayer is not for you getting what you want from God. It is for him getting what he wants from you.

You will also begin to comprehend that prayer is not searching, nor begging, nor pleading. It is rather opening up to the God who is already knocking at your heart door. This opening of doors, conscious doors and subconscious, is prayer at its very best. You make a great discovery when you sense that the first move of the divine-human encounter is God's move. He is constantly seeking lives where he can enter to glorify the earth with his love.

Learning to pray together takes time, as all good things in marriage take time. But it does make sense, doesn't it? God is love and you both believe he is the author of your union. So the more you create channels through which his divine love can flow into your human love, the greater your love will be.

It is important that you learn this and practice it together. It may be dangerous for one person to stand still while the other advances. Wedlock is not for widening the distance between two people. It is for closing gaps in their differences until these two separate lives cohere around a Holy Center which is life as it was meant to be.

What I am saying here is not mere theory. Time and again I have seen marriages which seemed utterly hopeless come to a newness of life through the practice of silent prayer together.

But I am speaking also from personal experience. It was a big job your mother took on when she walked down the aisle to take this hand and hear the preacher say, "Dearly beloved, we are assembled here to join this man and this woman in holy wedlock."

It was not long until she discovered that there were many warring selves she must bring together in this boy she had taken to raise. Her challenge was to draw a rough, scarred and woolly male into oneness with her inner calm, her softness, and her gentle femininity.

But you know how she did it, don't you? I watched her sitting there in the early morning with her Bible and her books. She called it her "quiet time," and I came to understand that her serenity of soul was the answer to my confusion.

Then one day in my desperation I asked her to lead me, too, "beside the still waters." So she took me with her to her school of prayer, and that's how I know firsthand that this is the key of keys.

Today, after twenty-six years of marriage, I am more sensitive to the thrill of her presence than I have ever been. When I come on her unexpectedly in a crowd, it is like a glad little song rising up somewhere inside me. When I catch her eye in public, it is as though she were hanging out a sign with the exact word of inspiration I need right then. When I drive home in the evening, I must consciously guard the foot pedal lest I step on the gas a bit too fast as I approach the house where she waits for me. I still count it the day's biggest thrill when she comes hurrying from wherever she is to greet me with a holy kiss and press her body close against mine in yearning. And as I look down the road ahead, I see an elderly man and woman going into the sunset hand-in-hand. I know in my heart that the end will be better by far than the beginning.

I could wish for Vincent no greater gift than this—that his wife might lead him, as her mother led her dad, to the secret chamber of divine communion where two lives are blended into a sacred trinity.

I hear some of the sociologists arguing that one solution to the marital breakdown of our times is to make divorce harder. That could help in some cases, but the real answer is not to make divorce harder. It is to make marriage what it should be. And what it should be is a sacred triune relationship between the Lord and you and your husband forever and ever.

Prayerfully,
Dad

What Is Your Happiest Memory?

What is the happiest memory of your marriage?

Interesting question, addressed to our ninety-year-old neighbor on her birthday. We called her Grandma Mac, and the whole neighborhood had gathered at her back porch.

Item one on the scene for some of us was a majestic three-tiered coconut cake. The centerpiece, with nine candles. ("Nine," whispered its creator, "because I thought she'd do better blowing out nine than ninety." Nice!)

But first there were presents, laughter, and fun, and as Grandma Mac unwrapped her gifts, someone asked her this pensive question: "Would you tell us what is the happiest memory of your ninety years?"

It did seem a natural question right then. So we stilled ourselves and waited.

What would she say?

What do you think she said?

(You should know that she'd been a widow for seventeen years. Because her husband was a career officer in the military, they had traveled the world together. "Several times clear around," she'd told us often. He'd also invested wisely, and that being true, she lived with another blessing. She'd been able to buy almost anything one little lady could want when she wanted it. Idyllic background really, for the recollection of memories.

But tonight there was no need for recollection. Without one moment's hesitation she said, "Oh, that's easy. It's all those times Louis and I would sit on the back porch and visit."

It *is* a pensive question, isn't it? What will our happiest memories be when we are ninety? One thing is certain for almost all of us—our happiest memories will focus on some kind of people-interaction.

Talking with that special friend. Hearing and being heard. Laughing together, crying, thinking together, and then some more plain old vanilla visiting.

It doesn't matter what we call it. By any name, at ninety years, or any time, memories at their warmest will glow with positive people recall.

This being true, we are brought to another basic question: What *are* the three most important words in any marriage?

"I love you"?
"You are beautiful"?
"Please forgive me"?

All ultraprime phrases for sure. But our nomination for the three most important words in any marriage will forever be:

TALK, TALK, TALK

And following closely:

LISTEN, LISTEN, LISTEN

In preparation for this anniversary edition of *Letters to Karen*, our editor asked us: "What secrets have you two discovered in the past twenty years? What do you know now you didn't know then?"

To which we reply with four more ultraimportant words:

Bible study in duet

We have heard it said that year five is the bad year in many marriages. Others point to seven or eleven. For us, every one of those first years had far too many negatives. Sometimes they came with shouting and crying and loud banging. Sometimes they arrived unannounced on padded feet, and these for us were the real uglies—hurt and a sense of rejection, anger and slow burning, feelings unexpressed. Without *talk, talk, talk ... listen, listen, listen,* there simply was no healing.

When we first began sensing that our love was heading for trouble, we made a decision. Since we weren't doing well by ourselves, we would ask the Lord for help. And in answer to our prayers, we were led to a program of Bible study for just the two of us. Since that time, we have shared our method with thousands,* and out of that sharing we know this for sure—there is no method, no technique, no system as effective as learning to communicate through the Word of God.

In the closing thoughts of *Letters to Karen,* we said that learning to pray together made a mighty difference in our marriage. This is still true, and it has been true through all our forty-seven years together. As we refined our Bible study to go with our prayers in duet, our love has reached heights we never dreamed possible for Charlie and Martha.

What does this say? From our experience, what is says is that *visit, visit, visit ... talk, talk, talk ... listen, listen, listen* are holy business. And for the believer, that does make sense, doesn't it? If God is Love as Jesus said, then this also has to be true:

The more we create channels through which His love can flow into our love, the greater our love will be.

No matter how it's done, this we wish for you:
That you may develop together
  your own unique love
    at its Eternal best—
May you find it,
  care for it,

* *Bible Study in Duet,* Charlie and Martha Shedd, Zondervan, 1984

keep open its path,
and never lose it.
So across the days, the weeks, the years,
may you too be able to say
with the writer of Holy Writ:
"God ... for His great love
with which He loves us...
Has made us live together with Christ...
*And seated us with Him in heaven."**

Charlie and Martha Shedd
Blue Ridge Summit, Pennsylvania, 1985

*Selection from Ephesians 2:4-6 (Lamsa)

She was pure joy and she could only create unhappiness by being absent!

(An anonymous tribute to a saint of the gentler gender.)

Letters to Philip

Contents

Preface

This is for Philip. I'm sure you'd like him right off if you met him. He'd put out his hand, turn on his million-dollar grin, and give you the feeling that he is genuinely interested in what's going on inside you.

He is. From the time he took his first toddler steps, he had as many friends as there were people up and down our block. He just naturally loves folks.

He also loves Marilyn and that's where I come in. A few weeks before their marriage he asked me in his best you-can't-turn-me-down style, "Dad, would you write me some letters on how to be a good husband?"

There may have been several reasons why he would make such a request. For one thing, he knows that by the very nature of my work I spend many hours with husbands and wives who aren't making a go of it. Then, too, prior to our daughter's marriage I wrote *Letters to Karen* and every parent wants to spread his attention equally.

But there was another more important reason why Phil would ask that I do this. He needed to know! Would you believe any virile young man could grow to adulthood these days without catching on that there are two sexes? Well, if anyone could, he did! Until he met Marilyn, I don't think he had given it a second thought that God created people male and female.

This incredible situation probably started that day when he stuck his finger in an empty light socket. Most three-year-olds give it one try and learn right there this isn't for them. But not Phil. The whole event seemed to turn him on. From that day to this he's had a passion for anything with wires, current, and how does it operate?

What would you do if your son's first grade teacher called to say that Junior had been cutting classes? Well, you'd probably panic, like we did. But after the first few times, if he was like Philip, you'd do some research on where the electricians were working in the neighborhood. Then you would make your way to wherever that was and there he would be, totally enthralled in the goings-on. Or, if it was lunch hour, you might find the little guy sitting on a box bombarding the elders with questions.

If you couldn't find him, naturally you would imagine all sorts of horrible things. But after a while you would get used to that too. So you would sit on the front steps and wait. Finally, here he'd come, staggering under a load of switch boxes, insulators, wires with all those pretty-colored strands, and a multitude of broken parts with which his heroes had loaded him down.

Then you would take him back to school, all the while explaining that he must get a *general* education. You would also wonder what to answer when he'd say, "But, daddy, my teacher is so dumb she doesn't know *anything* about electricity!"

Of course, it all came out fine, like so many things do in the raising of children. He became an expert ham radio operator and greater love for his hobby hath no man than one of these. It is a perfectly marvelous thing when this happens to a boy who couldn't care less about school. They say that a youth who has lost interest in general education is headed for trouble. But they also say there is no known record of a ham radio delinquent and I believe them. He wouldn't have time for devilment if he was learning Morse Code, drawing schematics, building receivers, and talking all night to someone in Russia on twenty-meter band.

He wouldn't have time either for girls, which is why I can say without equivocation that at least one boy I know grew to adulthood with very little thought about male, female, and such incidentals.

Then he met Marilyn. At first she was just another passenger in his car on weekends. They are attending the same junior college. (Three cheers for the Navy! During nearly four years in a sailor uniform *they* convinced him that a general education was worth pursuing if he could work it in with ham radio.)

Then suddenly Marilyn became *the* passenger. But after several weeks of bumping her shins on his mobile "rig," listening to him "Calling C-Q! Calling C-Q!" she said "Ouch" one day in a voice that came through over the ham radio chatter.

That sounds like a reasonable thing to say, but right there, according to her report, he stopped the car, looked into her pretty eyes, and say, "Baby, let's have an understanding. If this goes on getting serious between us, you better learn to love ham radio because if anything goes, it won't be all this good stuff!" (From which you can see that he already had a good start on how to clarify certain issues.)

But don't worry about Marilyn. She knows a thing or two herself. If you could see their cozy little apartment today, you would know that here is one woman who has discovered her man's wavelength and how to keep the message coming on. Any girl who can accomplish the miracle of making the living room look like home *and* a ham radio haven is worth treating extra-special.

So, that's why he asked me to write him like this. Then one day he suggested that we share these letters. Like he said, "Most of the guys I know want their marriage to be extra-special!"

Charlie W. Shedd
Houston, Texas, 1968

The First Letter:
Take Charge

Dear Phil,

The other day I saw an interesting plaque in one of our neighborhood gift shops. Some clever merchant was featuring it for Father's Day. The motto read:

WHEREVER DAD SITS
IS
THE HEAD OF THE TABLE

I hope it sells like crazy because this is one of the basic needs of every home. So, one of my first bits of advice on how to treat a woman is "*Take charge!*" For the good of your marriage, for the good of your children-to-be, and for the good of the nation's future I hope you'll read me loud and clear.

There are dozens of ways you might hear this: "Get control!" "Seize command!" "Run the show!" "Grab the reins!" "Call the signals!" "Stay at the helm!" "Steer your ship!" "Name the tunes!" "Bring 'em to heel!" "Sit on the lid!" Any variation will do provided you learn that there is a delicate line between "just enough" and "too much."

The image here is not that of a mighty potentate sitting on his throne, ruling his cowering subjects with an iron hand. This is more like a conductor standing on his box directing a symphony. Delicate, but definite! Subdued, yet powerful!

As you know, I see many marital problems from the inside. Some things you wouldn't believe. Others are downright funny. But in some the pain is awful and among the worst are those where the only right words are "Get your foot off the lady's neck, Hitler!

You can never win a woman's love by applying the hobnail boot."

What I am saying is that women hate dictators, despots, tyrants, and old meanies—but they respect strong leaders.

Here are three quotes from the feminine front to show you what I mean. Number one is the word of a successful lady editor.

"All day long," she says, "I make decisions. I talk with men, deal with men, compete with men. But at night I long to be all woman. It is so good to have a man who will open the door, order the meal, and give me the feeling that I can let down now."

The next witness is a sweet little wife whose husband obviously knows what he's doing. "Once in a while"—she smiles—"Tommy sticks his chest out and says, 'Now you listen to me, squaw! Get back in your wigwam. I'm the chief and don't you forget it!" On first hearing, you might think this borders on rough handling. But this is what she says:

"It's funny what this does. When he says it nice, I get the best feeling. You know, all secure, and like that!"

Number three is something else. This poor soul is at the opposite end of the problem. "Can you imagine how I felt?" she asks. "We were hardly home from our honeymoon when I saw clearly that Lawrence didn't need a home, he needed a nursery. Now don't get me wrong. I know every man feels like a cry baby some days and I enjoy mothering him once in a while. But all the time? When is it my turn?"

I could go on parading a long line of these. Some good. Some bad. But none quite as sad as the weary women who can't lean because there is nothing to lean on. Their men are too weak, too careless, too preoccupied, too much at the office, too long at their cups, or too something else to be the strong male figure at the head of the house.

Of course, like everything else, there are two sides to this story. Some juggernaut types may want their men to be submissive. But

I also know good women who took command because somebody had to march the troops and dad was too weak to do it.

So take it from me, your wife will love you more if she knows that you know when to stand up and say "Have no fear! Your leader is here!"

One reason why this makes a woman feel good is that she has what you might call a feminine mystique about the future.

Emotionally, most men are much more temporary than women. It is easy for us to believe that if everything is all right this minute then it's got to be fine tomorrow. But the female mind has an innate something that looks to this day and on down the road at the same time. To some extent, women judge what is happening now by the effect they think it may have on the years to come.

Since motherhood is a large part of a woman's career, she is continually measuring her man against the background of this question: "What kind of a father will he be?" So she is bound to love you more if you take charge early because you will have settled her questions about this.

On every hand she sees evidence that too many children are missing a strong authority figure. She knows some parents who are locked in a power struggle and the little ones are losing respect. She knows others where the roles are reversed, mother has won the battle, and the children are confused. Up and down the block, across town, and out in the country there are too many homes where father has abdicated and things are coming undone.

I don't need to tell you that some real psychological monsters are coming from somewhere. They are not nice to see, and any women who cares these days is saying to herself, "The world needs character. I want my children to be good citizens!" So when she looks at you as a father-to-be, what will she see? Does she smile or get a bit nervous?

You can see that all this reaches far into the future. That's why I say you mustn't delay. Take charge early and do it right.

How?

I can't tell you for sure. Nobody can. This is something you'll have to work out yourself. No two marriages are exactly alike. Because this is true, the blending of your two sets of strong points with your two sets of likes and dislikes is a unique challenge.

Yet you won't go far wrong if you shade away all the time from being a despot and move toward the idea of establishing your home as a democracy with a male head. We love our form of government partially because we feel it is a good balance between retaining some rights and delegating certain rights to other hands. And we are likely to love it most when we feel that our leaders are strong men, capable of good judgment in matters important to all.

In a sense, Marilyn has elected you to the high post of leadership in her heart and to head up your family. This gives you great authority and it is a high trust.

Don't forget that the kind of authority we're talking about here is the *authority of love!*

It seems to me that nearly every woman I know wants a man who knows how to love, with authority!

Lead on,
Dad

The Second Letter:
Learn to Be Kind

Dear Phil,

One day I came into my study through my private door to find a very attractive woman waiting for a visit. As I sat down in my chair,

I looked across the desk and felt that something special was about to take place. It was.

"I heard you say," she began, "that you would welcome some stories about ideal husbands. So I thought you should know about Mark. I think he is perfectly wonderful and I came to tell you why.

"From the day I started to school," she continued, "clear up to college, everyone made fun of my legs. As you can see, they look like tree stumps."

Then she stood up, and they did.

You would think she might be embarrassed to talk about herself like this. Actually, I feel a little that way as I look back on the incident. But she did it all so naturally. I remember admiring her sense of composure and thinking to myself, "This is *some* woman!"

"You know how children are," she said when she sat down to continue her story. "They can be cruel. Sometimes when I was little I would cry myself to sleep. As I grew older, I laughed with them to cover up. In high school I dated some but never more than a couple of times with any one boy and you can guess why.

"When I was a freshman in college I met Mark. I liked him right away. I felt so comfortable with him. Then he asked me to go steady and I could hardly believe it. He never made one single reference to my legs. But I did. You know, looking for assurance. Then one night he took my hands in his and said, 'Frances, I want you to quit knocking yourself. I love you the way you are. The Lord gave you good, sturdy legs. They give me a solid feeling and I like it.' You know what I did," she said. "I cried.

"Then one week," she continued, "he took me home, and when I met his mother I wanted to cry again. She was a cripple. She wore a shoe that was built up and she walked with a limp. So I looked at him and he looked at me and I think I loved him right then like nobody ever loved a man before.

"Do you know," she concluded, "that was thirteen years ago and now I can honestly laugh about my legs. Can you see why I say he's wonderful? There isn't one thing in the world I wouldn't do for Mark!"

She's not kidding either, Phil, and I'm sure you will sense that she isn't. Why? Because that's how God made women. They'll do anything in the world for you if you put them at ease about their faults; build up their strong points; and reach that high level of kindness which seems to say, "The blend is what I like. I love you for what you are *in toto!*" This is what the psychologists call "acceptance," and you'll find it a solid fixture in every solid marriage.

Whether it is sturdy legs, a "family nose," or any other physical eccentricity makes no difference. If you are going to be safe as a "take charge" guy you better educate yourself in the art of being kind.

I used the word educate because most of us are naturally self-centered. Whether this is an ancient self-preservation instinct from way back there, or fungus off the family tree, or something else doesn't matter as much as facing the fact that we have it. Whether this comes easier for women than for men might also be open to debate. Personally, I think it's tougher for us males. But from what I have learned in my own marriage, and seen in others, there are not many questions more important than this: "*Am I willing to train myself away from selfishness toward the point where I honestly care how the other person feels?*"

Here is one more sure thing you can count on about Marilyn—like all healthy women, she has in her makeup something which can't help responding to kindness.

Deal gently,
Dad

The Third Letter: Start at the Mirror

Dear Phil,

Do you remember the night you came home from school and asked, "Dad, what good is it ever going to do me to remember what Macbeth says to this babe?"

You will admit it's no ordinary question, and I couldn't think of a single intelligent answer. I'm sorry, because I did come up with some brilliant ones later. But you know how it is. Certain opportunities have only one chance. So I went blank and there went Shakespeare right out of your life.

It certainly was not that you didn't have what it took to get through senior English. It was that senior English couldn't get through you because nobody could convince you that it mattered. But ham radio did, and was I ever proud the way you put that transmitter kit together in two days and one night! (Straight, I mean, without sleep!) The man at the store said you might "mess it up permanently" if you did it alone. But you tied right into those two thousand parts and it worked perfectly the first time you turned it on.

That's how you have always been. You could do just about anything you wanted to do!

This is why I am especially glad for one thing you said when you asked me to write you. What you said was, "I want you to send me some letters, on account of I've got a lot to learn about being a good husband."

Over the years I have known many of our gender whose attitude was "If only *she* would change, things would be just dandy!"

Of course it isn't true that all the troubles will be your fault. Yet this is a fact you can count on: A wife is much more willing to face what *is* her fault if her husband has shown that he is willing to assume what is *his* responsibility.

So I am glad for your request and the way you put it. If you keep on developing this attitude, it will be a real asset in all your relationships.

One sure make of the "take charge" man worthy of his position is the greatness of soul that can look in the mirror and say "Here's where we begin!"

Keep humble,
Dad

The Fourth Letter: Ask Her to Help You Grow

Dear Phil,

One kind of praise from a husband is a real bell ringer in the heart of any wife. This is the kind that goes "I couldn't have done it without you!" or "I owe it all to you!" One reason why this can't miss is that the female has an innate longing to be of worth to the male. With the good ones you don't find much variance here.

Since you started at the mirror by recognizing that your part is to be a good husband, you have already put your foot on the next step up. This is where you tell your wife that you know you have faults and ask her to help you grow.

Acceptance with kindness does not mean that you must consider each other "just perfect." So you remember that there are *two* kinds of faults to be dealt with. There are those you can never remove. These you work into your love as props to the total structure. Then there are others which can be corrected and you mark yourselves as good stewards of life if you face these intelligently—together.

Naturally, this kind of thing requires a feel for the proper cadence. There are some days when we don't have the slightest hankering for self-improvement. Sometimes it takes all the strength we have just to go on breathing. Other occasions are not for analysis. These are for enjoying each other "as is." Some couples over-press. Some wives over-nag. The Lord knows I see enough top sergeant women already without adding to their corps by encouraging this in your home. But if you have conveyed the assurance that you will welcome her suggestions, she will learn to pace herself as a good wife should.

Of course you're smart enough to know that you don't begin this with the pronouncement "I accept the places where you can never be better! But there are some areas where you could improve considerably. Let us now consider together how to remake Marilyn!"

Obviously, that won't do. So as a wise husband you initiate your family fact-finding by saying something like this: "I love your accolades, but the truth is that I do have faults. Therefore, since I respect your judgment I am soliciting your help in making me a better man."

When sufficient time has passed for her to recover from the shock (both that you are *not* perfect and that she has married someone this honest), you can follow your opening slavo with another piece of news guaranteed to make her cooperate.

What you do now is to explain that *she can help you earn more* if she will take off her rose-colored glasses. They say that money talks, and this is one place she can hear it.

When she thinks this through she will realize that you're not kidding and she better not either.

I know too many men with odd habits, personality flaws, and peculiar little mannerisms holding them back. Here, for example, is a capable minister who was recently rejected for a top pulpit because he resorts to rolling his eyes up into the top of his head when he is talking with people whom he wants to impress. If you think it was a bit picayunish to hold him back for a reason so small, then you better believe me, it's not just the church where these things happen.

As a matter of fact, I've heard every one of the following given as excuses for not moving some man ahead in the business world: cracking knuckles, cleaning fingernails, dropping ashes, slouching, sucking through the teeth, chewing toothpicks, picking at an eyebrow, constantly crossing legs, steady patting at a wave in the hair. In the world of buying and selling—where money changes hands, or doesn't depending on personality reaction—things like this may determine whether a man goes up, goes down, or goes on at the same old level.

This is why you may have taken a long step forward when you educate your wife to be honest. When she offers various items for your improvement, I would train myself to make the first word of reply "Thank you!" Then when you are sure you won't argue, sure you won't pout, sure you won't retaliate, you can add "I didn't know I was doing that. You and I make a great team!"

This word "team" is another sure winner. As a matter of fact, I cannot recall a single situation in marital counseling in which either party was considering separation if they felt there was *any* improvement going on between them. But I can remember dozens who gave up because they knew their relationship was getting them nowhere.

"Incompatibility" is the most popular legal description of marital breakdown. In some cases it means these two people have grown tired of telling obvious little lies to each other. Their marriage has reached a sterile dishonesty and any future is better than that.

"Home" means so many things. Home is a haven, Home is for relaxing and letting down, way down. No front here, just "be yourself." But when home is at its best it is also a place where two people are sharing the thrill of becoming finer persons together.

There are limitless possibilities if you get your marriage moving in this direction. As we said at the beginning, a woman is so constituted that she longs to be worth something to her mate. So if you lead out by asking her to help you improve, if you receive graciously what she has to offer and thank her for it, one day she'll turn the whole thing around and ask you to help her! Why? Because she will sense that she is married to a growing man, and she will want to grow with him.

I don't need to tell you that society desperately needs folks who are pouring into the foundation the stuff of general betterment. People like this are the hope of tomorrow. You have done a great thing when you lead your marriage to the place where you can honestly say together:

"We not only aim to be good *to* each other, but *for* each other and the world."

Keep growing,
Dad

The Fifth Letter: Seven Goals for Communication

Dear Phil,

In the consultation room I hear women complaining about many different things, but high on the list is failure to communicate. For some little time now I've been gathering a collection of what I call "Sayings of Lonesome Wives." Here are three of the best examples:

"You've heard of the great stone face? Well, I married it!" ... "All I ever see of my husband at breakfast is a hand groping for his coffee from behind the morning paper!" ... "Would you believe it? My man can go for days on one word. To be perfectly honest, sometimes he says it twice to give it a different meaning. His total vocabulary is 'Uh!' and 'Uh! Uh!'"

What they are saying is that life gets downright grim married to a man who won't talk. It is true that some husbands never shut up, but for every one of these I know several dozen who err on the silence side.

The point I want to get over today is that this is no way to treat a woman. Unless a wife is some kind of zombie, she wants to know what's going on in the mind of her loved one.

This is especially important for a man to face because his role outside the home often moves him in the opposite direction. Anyone who has ever worked knows that part of the secret is to say "Yes, sir!" when you feel like saying "You, sir, are an old goat!"

Most men accept this as a natural part of earning their living. But it isn't natural. As a matter of fact, some psychiatrists say that this wearing of masks, living behind a facade, and burying our real feeling is nothing short of slow suicide unless we have some other outlet.

Against this background the art of verbal communication in marriage takes on special significance. In one sense it is a particular kind of life insurance. But it doesn't come cheap.

For one thing, it requires specific planning and the dedication of time in your daily schedule. Most couples would never believe that "talk" is one of the simple pleasures most likely to get lost in the shuffle. But it is. Babies and business, social engagements, committee meetings, P.T.A., television, ball games, trivia, emergencies—dozens, hundreds, thousands of things are a sinister threat to the art of communication.

In premarital consultation I always ask the young lovers how good they are at verbal exchange. Almost without exception they answer "This is one of our strongest points." But some years later they come complaining "He won't talk!" "She clams up!" By these and other plaints they indicate there is no more of the babble they both loved and counted among their blessings.

You are a wise young husband if you determine that this is not going to happen at your house.

Your mother and I had a tough time opening up to each other during our first months together. This surprised both of us. We hadn't noticed that there were vast expanses of inner withholding during the years of our courtship. But there were.

As we faced the problem together it became clear that my running from ghosts and her self-containment could lead to no good. So one day we decided to look the monster head on. We agreed to at least communicate on whether we could ever communicate all the way.

In studying just that much together we stumbled onto the fact that some of the reasons for our hesitancies were long gone.

(That, incidentally, is a great discovery. When you face the truth that you no longer need to be chained to your past you have taken a long leap forward.) So we pledged each other to *try* exposing a little here, a little there, by some definite rules which might have a positive effect.

This is how we came up with a simple covenant offered here in the hope that it might be helpful. You will understand this was never drawn up as a signed document. It was more like a quiet agreement. I list them for you just the way we wrote them on our hearts.

Our Seven Goals for Communication

1. *We will aim to be "best friends."* Since friendship is built on time spent together we will have no less than one good visit daily with each other. We will arrange our schedule for this and keep it high on the docket of each day's business.
2. *At least once each week we will go out together.* A dinner, lunch, or any occasion to read each other's souls is time well spent. We will not let the children, or company, or the budget, or a committee meeting, or the tyranny of "the musts" and "the shoulds" crowd out the time for each other.
3. *We make it a goal to be honest all the way.* Since this requires self-honesty first we will spend some time in healthy self-analysis. By reading, studying and discussion we will seek to understand how our personal histories are affecting our marriage.
4. *As an ideal, forty-eight hours will be our hiding limit.* But since absolute honesty cannot always meet a deadline we agree to this—if we are not yet able to shape our feelings in words, we will keep trying. We will admit that we are struggling inside and ask for continued patience.
5. *We will aim for total mercy and forgiveness.* We may question, but we will not condemn. We will seek a spirit between us

where confession is heard with tenderness. We will be thankful for a place where we can face what we are.

6. *We will respect each other's privacy.* We will not crowd or jam the works by over-inquisitiveness. Aware that what we hide may be damaging, we nevertheless extend each other the amazing courtesy of inner destruction. Because self-revelation must come from the inside we will not push.
7. *We will remember that mystery is a blessing.* Because it takes a lifetime to close all the gaps in the most perfect relationship we will be gentle. We will love to the fullest what is given today and expectantly wait for tomorrow.

It will be obvious why we call these goals. After that first leap forward, some of the road to heaven is bound to be slow going. To let someone into your heart can be plain awful. Sometimes it is scary. It brings up things we didn't know we had, and one of these is resistance. This is the psychological term for slamming the door, running away fast, and saying "Let's forget the whole business."

This is why so few people have what it takes to make it all the way through to genuine transparency. But you can, and if you do keep it moving with a loving hand you will one day reach those high levels reserved for brave souls who have been to the depths together.

I have known more than a dozen thrilling old couples who have reached their fiftieth anniversary and three who went as far as their sixtieth. They represented a wide range of income, employment, status, and influence. But they had one thing in common. Whether it was the weather-beaten farmer in Nebraska or the smooth-faced banker in one of our largest cities; the schoolhouse janitor in a crossroads town or the president of a great university—whoever he was, he and this woman beside him had learned how to share themselves with each other in total companionship.

That is a great word—companionship. It takes on added significance as the years pass. Sexual desires might fade and the need for excitement diminish. Money worries may subside and so could your other anxieties. But there is one thing that you must be sure is continually on the increase. This is the gradual opening of two hearts to welcome each other at the core of their beings. The surfacing of the real you is the secret to long life, inner health, and total communion.

Keep talking,
Dad

The Sixth Letter
If You Like It, Say So

Dear Phil,

There are three things I aim to do every day as husband:

1. Tell her I love her
2. Do something nice for her
3. Pay her a compliment

The truth is that this only *sounds* simple. But you try these as a regular discipline, and you will see that they "say" easier than they "do." And the toughest of these to remember may be number three.

Psychologists tell us that there are several reasons why we restrain ourselves at this point. In some cases, they say, the hesitancy comes from a basic hostility syndrome, which means that we're mad at the whole world, people are no darned good, so down with everybody! Or somehow we got the message that, since we ought to affect a little embarrassment when we receive compliments, why should we embarrass others by praising them?

But I think there may be a more basic reason why many of us husbands are stingy with kind words. This is because we're people, and the average specimen of the human species is naturally inclined to be selfish. We spend most of our time thinking about number one. We are too preoccupied with our own emotional feelings. We don't have the time, take the time, or make the time to consider what it would mean to the other person if we opened our faces to say a good word.

You can believe me, every woman worth the name is an addict for masculine approval. And the best way to let her know you approve of her is to tell her. There are all kinds of other ways to get the job done, but from the feminine point of view, voicing your likes is one of the nicest.

One reason she is bound to think so is this: Marilyn has many needs, but one of her greatest is to please you! If things are normal at your house chances are good she's thinking of you more than you're thinking of her! This is why, if you give her some pleasant things to think on, you're doing a good thing for her, for you, and for your future together.

The Bible says, "As a man thinketh in his heart, so is he." This also goes for a woman. If you give her a lovely idea of herself, that's what she will try to become. This is why it makes so much difference what you're telling her. The time finally arrives when she accepts your estimate of her as her estimate of herself. I've seen many an ordinary-looking woman grow into a lovely thing because her husband told her she was lovely. I regret to report that I have also seen some truly gorgeous women gradually fade away because they were no longer inspired from the one source that mattered most to them.

All of which leads up to six very important words:

IF YOU LIKE IT, SAY SO!

With that as a background, I give you now a few examples of compliments I've heard or used myself to good advantage.

"*You're not a woman, you're a memorable occasion!*" This particular one can produce—in several places—like you wouldn't believe. One place it produces is in the boudoir. Later on I'm going to write you my thoughts on sex and we'll go into greater detail at that time. I'll give you some more classic compliments for those occasions, but suffice it to say here that you would be smart to praise her body and let her know what you like about her physical makeup. This shouldn't be hard. Pick out those things that are particularly appealing and simply tell her how you feel about them. The color of her hair ... her eyes ... "Ah, that voice!" ... the sweep of her shoulders ... and you take it from there!

You can bet the family china on this—she will respond like just great, thank you, if you let her know that you think some part of her body is among nature's lovelier manifestations. I know men who attained what must be a genius rating at this because they schooled themselves well, forced themselves to get with it, and stayed right on the job till great things happened. One of these fellows is married today to a svelte thing who is of such dimensions that you wouldn't be normal if you didn't look twice. You wouldn't believe it, Phil, if you had seen them when they stood at the altar some fifteen years ago. Perhaps he had a hunch that under all that suet there was a beauty trying to escape. Some men like a challenge. They like to be heroes. At any rate, I'm telling you true, when they walked down the aisle from the altar (forgive me) I was sure that fifteen years hence she would look like a cross between the rear end of a bus and some Wagnerian soprano. It just goes to show you what wonders can be done by a man who knows what he's doing. But let's move to another kind of compliment women really go for.

"*Baby, your blueberry pie is all by itself!*" Do you realize, my dear boy, what a tremendous undertaking it is to serve a good meal? Planning, buying, preparing, cooking, setting the table, dishing up, and then the whole messy business in reverse when it's over. In fact, one good meal is such an accomplishment that for you to sit there, devour it, and then hurry on back to your TV game without ever saying a good word must be a mortal sin. Of course I'm not God and I don't know the answer to the old argument about whether there are major and minor evils. But I've had to get up a few meals from beginning to end, and if there *is* a difference then neglecting to compliment the wife on a good dinner must be a very major error.

There are some instances in which you'd be a fool to pass up a one-hundred percent return on your investment. This is one of them and just seven words will do: "That was a *great* meal! Thank you!"

One wise old codger gave me this interesting slant on food and a man's compliments. "With my method," he said, "she'll snap herself out of her blue moods and never know what happened. If I see she's feeling kind of down, I ask her to get up a dinner of all the dishes she does best. Then I suggest we invite the kids over. We sit there and brag how nobody ever fried a chicken or scalloped potatoes or put together a coconut pie with the extra-special touch Mom puts to it. By the time everybody has heaped up his plate with seconds and heaped up the praises with it, she's feeling great."

Naturally, this wouldn't work for everyone. But a man who stays alert to his woman's needs and keeps thinking can use her strong points to bless her soul. Maybe this is what the Bible means when it says, "Let her own works praise her in the gates."

Most women know what they can do well. You had better study

her specialties—and how to build them into your life together.

Now we come to a compliment that is all the go at every age and without fail: "*You just go on getting better all the time!*" If you don't think it, of course, you won't say it. But if you can't find anything you feel is an improvement, you're probably either going blind or you need to get busy. *Something* about her is bound to get better than it was a few years ago, or last week, or even yesterday. This kind of compliment always wears well, but there are a couple of instances in which it is especially appreciated.

(1) When she's been struggling for a long while to improve something, to overcome a fault, or to accomplish a difficult assignment; (2) When she moves toward middle age, old age, or whenever you sense that she senses she's not what she used to be. A woman will be forever grateful to the man who can make her believe it when he says "You just go on getting better and better."

By now you get the idea. I've given you a few special kinds of compliments worth mulling over. You will develop your own, and they are the very best. Some of these you wouldn't want anyone to know, but they do something special for both of you and they leave an especially warm feeling when you're apart.

Right there is something else your phrases of praise can do. They can give her something to remember when you're out of town, or away for the evening, or gone fishing, or just off to work. A clever husband can learn how to turn up the thermostat when he leaves so that everything is nice and cozy on his return.

I was just about to sign off when I remembered one thing more. If you ever notice her putting her back in a position to be patted; or if she has to ask you "Don't you think it becomes me?"; or if she runs to the mirror more than usual; or if in any other way the gleam seems gone from her eye, then you better get busy. It's too many "Ah's" ago since you set her heart singing.

Women are complicated creatures? Yes! But they are also simple souls who like simple things and one of the simplest they like is one of the simplest to give.

I know this isn't the best type of comparison, but it helps me to remember that Shadrach, our family airedale, will come clear across the yard for one pat on the head. The average wife is like that. She will come across town, across the house, across the room, across to your point of view, and across almost anything to give you her love if you offer her yours with some honest approval.

Hurrah for Marilyn,

Dad

The Seventh Letter: The Power of Suggestion

Dear Phil,

In a few moments I'm catching a plane for home. I've been up here on a speaking engagement and, like always, heading back is the best part. But I want to tell you something that happened this morning. It illustrates what I was trying to say in my last letter about the power of words to shape a woman's future.

I'd have to add now that the same thing goes for a man. When I was shaving this morning I caught myself singing, "From the land of sky blue water comes the beer refreshing! Hamm's the beer refreshing! Hamm's beer!"

Now you know it's a fact that I try to begin my day with thoughts from a higher source than somebody's brewery. Yet the barons paid their money and their money did the job. Last night I was listening to a ball game and by constant repetition they cut this little groove in my head where they wanted it to be.

You know also that I don't drink beer. But if I did, I bet it might be Hamm's. In spite of the fact that I vowed me a vow if I ever drank beer it wouldn't be their beer, it probably would. The truth is that I can't get this silly little ditty out of my mine—"From the land of sky blue wa-a-ters."

There's my plane call!

The point I wanted to make is this: If the power of suggestion can affect us like that from a source where we couldn't care less, what do you think it would do if we heard it over and over from someone we loved?

Teetotally yours,
Dad

The Eighth Letter: How to Tell Her What You Don't Like

Dear Phil,

Let's say now that there is something you would like to change around here. You don't want to fight about it because you have a hunch that there must be some better way to handle this one.

But you have decided that you've got to get it on the table. For your own personal peace and the future of your marriage in general the time has come to declare yourself.

What do you do now?

I have a simple rule, which I pass along today as the right approach to get these little items moving. That is the crucial thing isn't it, just getting started. If you keep your head and say a prayer you can usually handle further developments as they come along. So here's the rule:

BEGIN BY TELLING HER SOMETHING YOU LIKE!

Suppose it's the lipstick she's been wearing lately. It really does make her look ghastly, but be assured you won't get to first base if you exclaim "Oh no! You look like a streetwalker!"

You could actually get the job done quicker, and leave her feeling good about it, if you simply told her nicely that in your opinion that particular color somewhat diminishes her natural beauty.

You will readily see that you have done a couple of good things here. You have assured her that you like the basic Marilyn and you have played to one of human nature's strongest desires. This is the hope that we will be able to make the best possible appearance. That's how the Lord made us. We all want to impress to our maximum.

You will observe that this has almost limitless possibilities. For instance, let us suppose again. Say now she is one of those modest maidens who wants all the lights off when she disrobes for retiring. Is this the time to declare "For Pete's sake, Marilyn, did you come over with the Puritans?" Or should you say something like this: "My dear, with a body like yours ... "

Your mother says that since you are a chip off the old block you will now have fully grasped the lessons for today.

So that's about the size of it for now, except to add this: Never let anyone lure you into the trap of thinking that because she is a woman she is likely to fall for anything. It isn't so; the truth is that the female has more native intelligence about more things than the male. I hate to admit that, but, from what I've seen close up, it's the awful truth.

Yet though they may forever out-think, out-wit, out-surmise, and out-maneuver us, there are these certain places where you can get their attention every time. One of these is right here: *There isn't a woman in the world in her right mind who would flatly reject any suggestion that might solidify her relationship with the man she loves!*

Psychologically speaking we are so put together that we are most likely to act on the advice of people if:

1. We respect the source of this suggestion as a person of wisdom (you know she thinks you're smart because you chose her).
2. We care about our relationship to this individual, and we would like to strengthen it.
3. Their thoughts for our improvement are presented in a positive manner that makes us feel good before we have a chance to feel bad.

Positively,
Dad

The Ninth Letter: Winning By Losing

Dear Phil,

We have spent a good deal of time discussing things that can be talked through. But chances are you will also have some things requiring a different approach.

Let me tell you about one very wise husband I knew and how he used a strategic retreat to accomplish his long-range goal.

It seems his wife's aunt had given them a Victorian vase that had been in the family since "Henry the something or other." He said the only way he could describe it was that it looked like somebody's ski accident. She said it looked to her like a rare and elegant heirloom. To him the colors were lurid. For her they were perfectly gorgeous. (Like I said, it was from her family.)

But whatever else it was, the thing *was* huge and that was the problem. She insisted on keeping it as the focal point in their parlor. This happened to be on one of those large, low coffee tables. It stood in the center of the room because it just didn't look right anywhere else.

For a long time this monstrosity seemed to dominate everything in their home. It also dominated their conversation. Actually he said even their evenings were built around the question "What else shall we do tonight besides argue about the ski accident?"

Now this man was some thinker, so he finally caught on. By his own admission he was being a clumsy husband and getting nowhere with these tactics. So he determined to back off and probe deep.

He could do it, too. He ran a big business, with many employees and daily decisions that called for sheer wisdom. He prided himself on his ability to manage men, encourage salesmen, evaluate markets, and see the numerous sides to every situation.

After applying his thinker to "the ski accident," he decided on a plan. One night he went home and suggested that this very evening they should rearrange the living room.

"Oh no you don't!" said she. "I know what you're up to! That vase will not budge! It's a valuable piece of property, delicate heirloom, etc., etc."

But much to her surprise, he said, "Lillian, I'm sorry I've been so stubborn. I resign. Let's leave it where it is and arrange the room around it."

When she had picked herself up from the floor and recovered her strength sufficiently, they set out to accomplish just what he had planned. After all, when a man capitulates that much, a woman can hardly say "No" to a simple request like moving the furniture. Besides, she always enjoyed these times. They did it rather regularly. It was one of their favorite games.

Right here I should tell you a little more about this couple. They loved their home as few people I've known. It was beautiful. They also loved each other dearly and that was beautiful too. Their favorite pastime was sitting together after dinner—reading, talking, sometimes holding hands, sometimes saying nothing, sometimes discussing little things and big things about their day and about each other.

Now, here comes the smart part. Being the ultra in management, he maneuvered the various pieces so that "his" chair was directly opposite "her" spot on the sofa. And between them was "the ski accident" ("elegant heirloom").

He said that he sensed he might win from the very first night. In the middle of her reading, as she was wont to do, she commented, "Harry, did you read this about ... ?" Then she craned her neck to see if he was listening. He craned his, too, and assured her he was.

That's how it went for some time. Of course, he employed other "vase movers" as he called them. Sometimes he would say, "Do you know, my dear, there is nothing I like to do better than to sit here in the evening and look at you?"

"I like you, too!" she would say, peering around the vase.

Then, naturally, there were times when one of them would move from his side to her side and vice versa, so they could do what I have already told you—hold hands and things like that. On several of these journeys around the table one or the other, sometimes dragging a newspaper, nearly upset her treasure. (He vows he never did it on purpose and I suppose he didn't. This was an honorable man.)

Why didn't they move his chair? I wondered so I asked him. He said it was on account of the light cord and because they both like it where it was.

You've already guessed the outcome. One day, some weeks later, he came home and where do you suppose the vase was? In the dining room, on the floor, back in a corner.

He confessed that he almost made a terrible mistake. He started to say, "Oh I see you've … ." Then he caught himself in time. "Oh I see," he said, "you've got your hair up! That's how you wore it the first time I saw you. I like it that way."

I asked him if they ever discussed the vase again. "Heck no!" he almost shouted. "Why should we?" (It hardly seems possible to me that a man could be that noble. How could he keep from bringing it up at least once to gloat a little? But some men have more of whatever it takes to be that noble than I have.)

Anyway, I couldn't think of one reason why they should discuss it again other than to revel a bit.

I have sometimes wondered where the vase is gathering dust today. Is it in the attic, basement, or the hall closet? Knowing him, I'm sure she's the one who finally put it wherever it is. And knowing them both, I'm sure they're still sitting there in the evenings—reading, talking, and exchanging their glances with nothing obstructing. And knowing her, I'm sure she must smile sometimes and thank the Lord for a good man who could manage so much so well, but most especially that he would manage her with the deft touch of a wise husband.

I wonder who coined the phrase "I can't win for losing!" Whoever he was, he didn't know one thing. In marriage sometimes you get what you want tomorrow by yielding some ground today.

Keep thinking,
Dad

The Tenth Letter: Fragments of Devotion

Dear Phil,

Everyone agreed that Joe was a super-sorry husband. It wasn't that he drank, or gambled, or ran around with other women. But what kept the neighbors talking was the way Ann had to earn the family living. Year after year she sat behind her desk in the lumber-yard office while Joe kept floundering around.

He always had the biggest plans. Any time you met him he would be talking up a storm about some fabulous new line he had just taken on. In the years when I knew them, he sold (for a short time each) fire extinguishers, vitamins, vacuum cleaners, burglar alarms, home freezers, burial insurance, mutual funds, diet aids. These he handled intermittently between what he called "my new position as official representative" (for a short time each) of a Rocky Mountain children's camp, a Midwest denominational college, a do-it-yourself course in auto repair, a novelty line of western wear, a chain of health studios, and a photography specialist in children's pictures (the kind with the pony).

So all over town they kept saying, "Did you ever see anything like it?" or, "Wouldn't you think she'd get her fill of him?" or, "Why in the world does she take such treatment?"

Then one time she had an emergency operation and in the days of her recovery I learned another thing for sure about women. This is that THE LITTLE THINGS PAY THE HIGHEST DIVIDENDS!

Being a man, I am prone to think that it's got to cost, like a mink stole, a new car, or at least three dozen roses ... but this is not so. What a woman likes is the fragments of devotion small items, inexpensive gifts, any humble gesture which seems somehow to say that she has what it takes to keep a man enamored. I also learned that with woman *what it means* matters a whole lot more than what it costs or how long it lasts.

How I got the message was that every day Ann welcomed me to her hospital room with a beaming report of what Joe had brought her the night before. The record went something like this:

Monday	A jigsaw puzzle from the dime store
Tuesday	The latest issue of her favorite magazine
Wednesday	Three large yellow apples
Thursday	A seventy-nine cent box of stationery
Friday	Bouquet of wild flowers (he had driven to the country to pick them)
Saturday	Some perfume from the corner pharmacy

Sunday, Monday, Tuesday, Wednesday of the next week—other little remembrances of the same variety.

"Good old Joe," she would say, "I feel so lucky the way he spoils me! He's always been like that! So thoughtful! So kind! He's a real genius at these things!"

All of which says what? Which says that a woman will take a whole lot—people's talk, family criticism, hard work—she will put up with all this, defend her husband vehemently, and count herself lucky if she figures him for an expert in the little matters of devotion.

There are several ways you can develop this art of extra thoughtfulness. In this letter I'm going to tell you some things I have found helpful in the hope that they may aid you as you school yourself in this direction.

For one thing, *make something special of the special days.* One of the happiest couples I know celebrates in some manner on the twenty-ninth of each month. That's the day they were married and they make it "theirs" by going out for dinner; or they have some little celebration at home; or he remembers her with a gift; or she does; or they both do. If this strikes you as overdoing it, you ought to hear that husband's witness. He claims that this monthly expenditure is worth every cent it costs, and all the memory effort it takes twelve times yearly.

Engagement anniversaries, first-date anniversaries, special anniversaries; remembering these and playing them up as extraordinary will be paid back many times over out of a woman's heart. A whole host of men never give these things one extra thought, although it would make them something special in *her eyes* if they did.

Another thing to remember is that *women go for ingenuity.* The little secret things between you; the games you play in your courting; the happy surprises she wasn't expecting—these tell her many things. One thing they say is that you are putting her high on your agenda, and this has to be good. You are thinking of ways to please her, and a woman will glow inside when she knows you've secretly been planning her happiness.

Let me give you an example of one man's ingenuity and how it works to advantage in their marriage. I heard this one day at the golf course. We were discussing "golf widows" and the men were bemoaning their wives' complaints. This fellow listened them through. Then when the time was right, he said, "You never hear my wife cry, do you? The reason is we made a deal. When I play on Saturday, I take her to dinner that night. This way she's got something to look forward to. I even notice now that she feels sort of bad when I don't play!"

So maybe this is kindness with a hook in it. Agreed that he's getting something for himself by giving her something. But the fact is, she doesn't mind. She likes it. All of which means that, with a little inventiveness, life together can offer many challenges for making things nicer both ways.

Here's another little secret you will do well to keep in the forefront: *Women go for some practical devotion.*

Questions, questions: Am I assuming my share of the work load at home? Am I hurrying off to the paper, to the television, to anywhere when I could take a few minutes to give her a hand? How long has it been since I surprised her by doing one of her jobs without telling her?

A middle-aged widow gave this interesting testimony one night in my hearing. Her husband had built up considerable holding in real estate. They had a summer home, a winter home, and they had traveled far and wide. All this had given her plenty to think about. But when it came to naming her favorite memory, she told about a small thing he did when they were just starting out. "Every Tuesday night when the children were little," she said, "he would let me go shopping alone while he babysat." Then she concluded, "I guess nobody but a young mother would know how I feel about that."

Words are important, and so are the special little gestures of fondness. But sometimes down-to-earth loving action is exactly what is needed to get the message through that you care.

We have said before that you had better spend some time trying to think like a woman thinks. If you do, you will discover why all these things mean so much to her. One of the strangest bits of feminine logic going on in a woman's head is something I find hard to explain. The best way I can put it is that, although she wants you to feel secure with her and she wants to feel secure with you, *she still hopes that you will keep on pursuing her even after you have won her!*

The male intellect differs here in that we are likely to reason "Well, now that's done! What's next?" The female, on the other hand, doesn't think that way. With her, this is more like our family story about Bach. You remember?

This young pianist had completed her first year at the conservatory. When her old professor at home asked her what they had accomplished that semester, she answered, "Thank goodness, we finished Bach!" Whereupon the aged sage replied, "My dear, nobody ever finished Bach. You may turn Bach off, but you never finish him!"

This is how love is to a woman. The man may think when he says "I do" that he has accomplished his mission. His wife, being much wiser about these things, senses that true love has no maximum. For those who keep opening new roads into each other's heart each day and very often, new possibilities are forever opening up and the greatest love goes on to new greatness.

I suppose this is why I have never heard one woman complain about her husband being too considerate. I am wondering if there is any woman anywhere who ever go too much affection? I doubt it. They're not made that way. All the good ones I know have an endless capacity for devotion and tenderness and the little things.

Never quit courting,
Dad

The Eleventh Letter: "I Can Hardly Wait to See You"

Dear Phil,

Before we go further, it might be well for me to remind you that I have a high regard for your basic integrity.

Some of these facts I'm telling you about female reactions could be downright dangerous without a wholesome sense of honor. But the fact that certain base fellows use love's secrets ignobly shouldn't keep men of character from making life interesting where it ought to be. And God knows one place where it ought to be is in the husband-wife relationship.

So, here goes with another truth you have a right to know. This is that *nothing can turn a woman on quite like knowing that she turns you on*. Something inside the most lady-like lady will respond with excitement if you find her exciting.

Those husbands I know whom I count most successful put something into their love life that seems to say "How lucky can I be to live with a thrilling woman like you?"

I take it for granted that you will begin right here—be sincere! Don't ever tell a woman something she can interpret as superficial flattery. Unless it's one of those days when you're kidding each other and you both know it, you had better keep your love-making within the range of plausibility. But you can count on it that this is a wide range. If you give her only those things she can believe, you've still got plenty of room to make life interesting.

One thing she can accept as authentic is your assurance that you miss her when you're not together and that you are looking forward to being with her again. Anticipation is a big item in the most vibrant marriages. This is sure to have the feel of the real to her because you are only continuing the way you felt when you were courting.

Don't ever lost this "I can hardly wait to see you" spirit, which was such a big part of your life together before marriage. Do you remember how it was when you came home from college? You drove right past our house and hurried on to see Marilyn. Those twenty-four extra miles (when you multiply by two) meant a lot to her. They told her more than a thousand words. Your excitement kept her excited.

Too many couples let this get away. But this is unfortunate, because they have dropped one of the most certain ways to maintain the zest in their love life.

With a little practice, you can keep the enthusiasm at high pitch and it will be worth everything to both of you. All over the place there are dozens of instruments offering themselves as aids to the husband with imagination.

One of these is the telephone. Mr. Bell did a great thing for us men when he invented this little gadget. Use it often. Call her up and tell her you're looking forward to getting home. Or when your work allows, invite her to meet you somewhere. Words like this have a special ring for feminine ears: "I've got a gap in my schedule here and I'd sure like to spend it with you! Come on down and let's have a bite together." At least one woman I know can get just as excited over a hamburger and the royal treatment at lunch as she does over a dinner in one of those restaurants where the cost for two is equivalent to the monthly payment on the car.

I find it a good procedure also to check now and then on the impression I must be making when I first get home in the evening. Perhaps I am unduly aware of this because when I'm calling on parishioners I get into many homes late in the afternoon. Often while I am there, father comes home.

There are more ways to make re-entry into the family than you could possibly imagine. If the children head for the bedroom and mama starts to stiffen, you know what that means. But if the little ones go for the door and the Mrs. begins to glow, then this little drama says a whole lot. What it says is that here is a man who is good company. This man is wanted. To be wanted at home is a high aim for all of us men.

We have said before that it doesn't always take big things to get us to our goals. Sometimes the little ones matter most. So, if I were you, I would keep checking. Are you giving her the impression that you've been thinking of her with anticipation and counting on what's going to happen between you? You can do it by telephone, or cablegram, or by the simple little telegraph of a look exchanged.

Here's something else I'd learn to work into your love life. Let her catch you now and then looking at her expectantly. Or brighten your expression when you see her looking at you. These can be every bit as effective as giving her the impression that you've just floated in over the housetops to see her.

I have heard it rumored that the French are the lover *par excellence*. This is a little verse from over there that goes, *"Je t'aime plus qu'hier moins qué demain."* In our language it reads:

I love you more than yesterday,
Less than tomorrow!

With every nationality and in any language the spirit of that verse goes exceedingly well with women. You can take it from one who has found it is true—you do a great thing for your life together if you keep your love looking forward with high hopes.

Expectantly yours,
Dad

The Twelfth Letter: "Late" Is a Four-Letter Word

Dear Phil,

When the roll is called up yonder, some folks are sure to be late. Now, tardiness is *not* a greater sin for male than female, but you should know that most wives think it is.

Some of the gripes I hear in marital consultation go like this: "He *always* keeps me waiting!" ... "We *never* get anywhere on time." ... "He thinks he can show for dinner any old hour he pleases!" ... "Why can't he let me know when he's held up at the office?"

These are only a few selected at random from dozens more like them. The truth is that I've heard just as many from men. But let's stick to our subject and see how it applies from the husband's side.

Why does it bother a woman when her man is constantly behind time? Like almost everything else in marriage, there are many reasons: (a) we said in our last letter, the feminine mind thrives on thoughtfulness; (b) being a lady, she can't help wondering what *really is* holding you up; (c) you used to be prompt in your courting days ... what's the matter? ... is she slipping?; (d) do you need vitamins? ... minerals? ... something else you're not getting?; (e) dilatory men do not make good livings; (f) many other thoughts from minor irritation to major panic.

We could go on for a long while hammering away at this theme, but the telephone is ringing off the wall, and I've got to be going. It might even be one of the good gals of the parish wondering why her pastor takes so long to answer the phone. So we'll let it go at that for this letter.

Only, I thought it might be well to remind you that in checking over your arrival technique, you would do well to include this thought: Most women appreciate a man who gets there on time most of the time and when he can't she knows that a phone call seldom costs more than a dime. Ten cents isn't much for a woman's peace of mind.

Don't ever forget that a contented wife who knows her husband has been thinking of *her* feelings is worth every cent of whatever it costs to be considerate.

Hurriedly,
Dad

The Thirteenth Letter: How to Treat a Woman in Public

Dear Phil,

Do you remember the lovely compliment paid to some saint of years gone by?

She was pure joy and she could only create unhappiness by being absent!

After observing for twenty-one years, I'm sure you'll agree this is an accurate description of how your mother affects people. Of course I'm her husband and you're her son so some might say we are prejudiced. But among even her casual acquaintances everyone knows the lady glows.

Would you believe she hasn't always been like this? She would be the first to tell you that in the early days of our marriage she was painfully bashful. In fact, there were more times than I care to recall when I actually felt sorry for her. She was that self-conscious.

The man who launched this amazing transformation was Judge Evans. He was a gentle, gray-haired barrister who lived up the street from our house, and for some reason he took a liking to me.

The judge always knew a need when he saw one, so in the weeks before our wedding he took me down into his basement study and gave me the business.

Of course I don't remember everything he said in the several times he did this, but there was one note he kept playing over and over. He gave me plenty to think about concerning proper deportment in every room of the house. Yet he was continually pointing to the outside door and telling me that a marriage is only as good as what happens in public.

"From marsupial to mammal," he would begin (this was one of his favorite expressions), "the average male seems to forget everything he knows about courting when he leaves his own doorstep.

"This is nothing short of stupid. Why? Because he's missing one of the best bets the Lord ever gave a man to make his wife utterly, totally, yes I would even say helplessly, in love with her husband."

You will recognize by now that the judge had the makings of a magnificent courtroom lawyer, which he was. Before he became a judge he could hold a jury spellbound, and that's what he did to me. So I listened, because I enjoyed it, but also because I knew that he knew what he was talking about. (Mrs. Evans was a little woman. She wouldn't weigh one hundred pounds with the groceries under her arm. But was she ever something! She literally shone, and that's not bad for seventy plus, which is what she had to be. He was almost eighty and they had been married fifty-eight years.)

"Since you are about to marry," he would say, "you might as well do it right. That means keep your head screwed on when you're with your woman in public."

Then he would reach for his water glass and take a slow drink, as though he was giving the truth some time to settle. When he was sure it had he would lean over his desk to deliver the clincher.

"You can take your place with the great ones," he concluded, "if you make a list of the things I've told you and keep adding to it. This takes time and takes some doing. But you better do it. You'll never be sorry if you make her think she is strictly first class in the home, and even more classy in public."

So I took him at his word and here is the list. Some of these things are straight from him the way I remember them. Others I got from observing. A few are my very own and you can improve on these. But whatever you do, promise yourself today that you will do what the judge says: "Keep your head screwed on when you're with your woman in public."

Here is the list:

1. When you enter the room, take her arm and come in smiling. If you look happy, she will, and God knows the world needs encouragement.
2. Walk proud! Act like you are thinking "How could I be so fortunate?" If you stick out your chest she will too. Most women look better that way.
3. Say something nice when you introduce her. I mean about her. This is good practice and it lifts her spirits. If you make her feel good, you feel good also.
4. When you sit down to dinner, hold her chair! Then pat her on the shoulder and smile. Keep smiling till she looks up. She'll soon catch on and it becomes a ritual. This is a very good thing.
5. When the conversation lags ask her a question! Be sure you choose one she can answer. Make it one of her favorite subjects and always wait for her reply. Never forget, smart people make others feel smart.
6. Never, and I mean never, fuss over little points in her story. Who cares whether the roses were true pink or only a faded

red? If she is all wrong, somebody else can set her straight. But not you.

7. After dinner, if you get separated, look her up once in a while. Be sure she is pleasantly situated. Tell her you missed her and is she all right?
8. When you are ready to go, hold her coat, take her arm, and open the car door for her! Not many men do and she knows it. This makes her somebody special.
9. On the way home take her hand and tell her how proud you were to have her along. A very good procedure. It pays off later.
10. Sometime when you are with her mother alone, tell *her* how much you appreciate her daughter. No woman alive could keep this to herself, and nothing does more for your wife than a compliment coming in sideways!

So there they are and I hope you will find them helpful. I've passed them along to many men, and where they put them to work I've seen them do wonders.

You need a charmer by your side? Of course you do. What man doesn't? Well, you can have one. Ten years from today, or thirty, if you do the job right you will have a wife who is strictly first class—"first class in the home, and even more classy in public."

Wake the town and tell the people,
Dad

The Fourteenth Letter: How Not to Treat a Woman

Dear Phil,

If I am to do a thorough job of filling your request, it will be necessary now and then to come at our subject from the back side.

Under the general theme "How *Not* to Treat a Woman" I can give you some prime examples from two sources: the embarrassing personal memoirs of yours truly, and a gathering of goofs that I call my "husband-lulu" file.

From time to time in our letters I will be drawing on both of these. Here, let me present one of the prize illustrations of why women cut their wrists and drown themselves in bathtubs. It is also why they leave notes that read "Dear John, I have gone away with Herbert. Good-bye." Fortunately, that didn't happen here, but some women are made of very stern stuff.

This one was. She came into my study looking for all the world like she had just dedicated her life to getting even. The reason she looked that ways is that she just dedicated her life to getting even.

She had been in a automobile accident five days before. Some women go all to pieces at times like this. Others, bless their hearts, experience a sudden rush of good judgment. So, being one of the latter and a dutiful wife, as soon as she could, she phoned her husband.

Now what should a man do *first* if that happens?

Of course, you're right! But that's not what he did. Instead, he asked, "How much damage did it do to the car?" (Well, it was a practically new Oldsmobile.)

Query number two was, "Whose fault was it?"

You know that we all sound unsure of ourselves part of the time and particularly when our nerves are shattered. So, since her answers did not suit him, he gave her explicit instructions. (Obviously, one of those guys who thinks of all the angles *except* the right one.)

His third offering was this little gem: "Listen, darling, do not admit one thing! You phone the insurance company and I'll call the lawyer. Do you understand what I mean?"

She understood.

Then, to show you that even an idiot can do some things right, he added, "Just a minute and I'll give you the insurance number!"

"Thank you *so* much!" she said. "Aren't there *any* more questions?"

"No!" he replied, "I think that about covers it!"

"Oh, *does* it?" she shouted. "Well, just in case you're interested, I'm at the hospital with five broken ribs."

Question: How can a man effectively say "I'm sorry" after a thing like that?

Answer: He can't, effectively!

Of course I suppose in his behalf it should be noted that he *knew* the accident was not fatal. Dead wives do not make phone calls.

All this was several months ago and I am pleased to report that their union is beginning to solidify once more into something resembling a marriage. He's told her a thousand times he's sorry, and you believe he means it. But to borrow a line from the psychologists' report, "The prognosis is somewhat guarded," which in layman's language, means "If I were you, I wouldn't bet on it."

What is the lesson for today?

Lesson: *Always, without exception, every day, all week, the whole year, permanently, with no variance, and I mean one hundred percent of the time, the female of the species responds best if she knows she is number one on some male agenda!*

Naturally, the most direct way to get this across is to tell her. "Verbal assurance" is the term and there are not many wives who can get too much of it.

"Aw, but this sort of thing isn't my strong point!" How many times have I heard them say it? Meanwhile, back at the bungalow, the lady wonders. Don't let her do that. One way or another, you must get the message through that first, last, and foremost, she's number one.

So it still doesn't sound right? Okay. This doesn't need to come by way of the lungs. Women can also read sign language. Sometimes a look or a touch or a gesture is better than a thousand words.

I know one husband who got his point across this way: He never took off his hat when he came home until he kissed his wife. Even if she was on the phone, out at the clothesline, or back in the children's bedroom, he would look her up and deliver his message.

What did he do if they had company? For an answer, I quote what she told me. "One of the biggest thrills of our first year together was the time his mother came to see us. It was her first visit. When Peter came home that night, do you know what he did? He walked right past his mother and kissed me. Then he turned and kissed her. Then he took off his hat."

Without saying a word, he had let them both know how things stood. He had also established his standing with her, which was way out ahead with the great ones.

I can see you knitting your brow and wondering "How does all this 'she's tops' treatment fit in with the 'head-man' theme?" Actually, there is no inconsistency, not even a small one. They go together so well that, in the better marriages, where you see one you'll see the other. What happens is that you can be the leading man of her household *only* if she is the leading lady of your heart.

Of course she doesn't mind your giving some thought to other things. In fact, she hopes you will. She doesn't want you working with all those wires and parts and electrical currents unless you concentrate on what you're doing. But you had better convince her one way or another that these things run a poor second to her.

Like the guy who missed his cue when his wife broke her ribs, you can be a real stumble-bum if you fail to do this. Or like the man who kept his hat on, you can be a real genius if you let her know that everything else, including your mother, comes second to her!

First things first,
Dad

The Fifteenth Letter: Treat Her as a Person

Dear Phil,

Today's story is about a rapidly rising young executive whose wife first came for help three years ago. She said that she had been watching her husband's climb and she had this queer feeling. It seemed that, as he moved toward the top, her love moved in the opposite direction. Now it was nearing the bottom and that's why she came to see me.

The whole thing was too bad, because they had an excellent start. He was devoted and she responded. They had fun, friends, and a fine future. He signed with a going company, they bought a nice house, and life was great by any measurement.

Then, like a true young comer, he began to be promoted. There was a raise in salary and then another and another. Now he was on his way and it looked like nothing could stop him. Even she couldn't, when she sensed he was heading away from things they had agreed were important.

Finally their whole life was built around his business success. Then one night something happened that prompted her seeking outside help.

He bought her a diamond necklace. It was very expensive, and you would think that any woman might thrill to its beauty. She did, too, for something like thirty seconds. But as he was fastening it about her neck, he made one of his now familiar speeches. What he said was:

"Baby, the man you live with has just been promoted to vice-president. In order that you might always remember this day, I decided to buy you this necklace. In case you are wondering as to its value, I want you to know this little dandy cost me exactly one half of my first year's salary!"

That, she said, was the sum total of his presentation. There was not one word about how much he loved her, how he appreciated her help, how beautiful she looked—nothing whatsoever, except this ode to his own ego.

(Before we go on, let me put in this little parenthesis. Whenever you buy her a gift, let *her* tell *you* how nice your gift is, while *you* tell *her* how nice *she* is!)

His next scintillating observation came in the car that night on their way to the company ball.

"You know how it is, baby! The new vice-president has to have class! They expect it! That's what they want! Then, we'll give them class, won't we? Yessir! Real class! I can hardly wait to see how they take it!"

So they waltzed and they rhumba'd and they danced the fandango. Great evening, for him. Numerous congratulations on his new position and a few on the necklace.

En route home he concluded his carnage with this monologue:

"You know what I was thinking, baby? I was thinking what an impression it made. Did you see how it sparkled under the lights? Why even old J.B. was giving it the once-over. I'll tell you what, baby, it's a symbol! That's what it is, a symbol! We're on our way and nobody can stop us! Yes sir! Just like I say, we're on our way ...." etcetera, ad nauseum.

That was three years ago, and she says she doesn't care now. She wants out. He says he would like to hold it together. She says that's phony, too. It may be. The other day while the three of us were viewing the wreckage, he mused, "What will they think at the company?" I'm sorry she heard that, but I guess it wouldn't matter. All these months she has felt like a billboard, until the love in her heart has just hauled off and quit.

Success! They call her "The Bitch Goddess," and that is an accurate title. She crosses the path of every ambitious man, and when you see her swaying skirts on the road ahead you remember I told you this is one sinister dame!

How are you going to protect yourself against this subtle danger? One way to do it is to keep saying, and meaning it, "I love you because you're you!" These are among the sweetest words ever to fall on a woman's ear. And the reason is that she wants to know that you know *she is a person, not a thing!*

Things are to use. People are to love. Be sure it's not vice versa with you.

Keep checking,
Dad

The Sixteenth Letter: A Half-Dozen "Nevers"

Dear Phil,

"Never say never again again" are the words of a song too old for you to remember, but before we leave the "how-not-to" theme, I'm going to say "never" an even half-dozen times!

Some of these are re-emphasis of things we have already discussed and others will be sounded again as we go along. If ever you feel we should push up the record and get on with it, you can be sure that the recollection of my own clumsy moments would indicate some things need repeating. I have seen these error so often in working with troubled marriages that I know they can be too easily forgotten.

Previously, we discussed opening up to each other in verbal sharing. You will observe that most of today's items center on what not to say. Some wag put it well when he said, "God gave man a mouth that closes and ears that don't, which should tell us something." That's a good word for husbands.

So here we go with "A Half-Dozen Nevers," which I wish somebody had told me for my first years as a husband.

1. Never point in derision to something she can't change.

Like we have said before, it is a smart man who decides some things once and for all. One such should be his personal decision never to throw up to his woman the things she can do nothing about. You will recall the story of Frances and how her husband worked those over-sized legs into his love to win her undying respect.

Don't ever forget it. The dictionary says that sadism is "cruel abuse of others," and there is nothing more cruel than hurling hurtful words about things which can never be changed.

2. Never criticize her in public.

You have noticed that certain couples make a sinister little game of slapping at each other when they are in the presence of others. Here are a few sample swats I've heard lately: Husband: "Thanks for inviting us over. This is *such* a welcome change from TV dinners!" ... Wife: "Why doesn't John fix it? That'll be the day. He doesn't know a saw from a sawhorse." ... Husband: "You better tell *me!* Jennie could get lost with a police escort!" ... Wife: "Did you hear that, dear? Andy bought Jean a new Buick. *He* must be doing all right!"

This trotting out each other's weaknesses beyond your own

door is always in poor taste. It is acutely embarrassing to innocent bystanders; it indicates that you have not been surfacing your rancor in an intelligent way at home; and the only thing it can possibly produce between you is a desire to get even.

You must remember that with women some things are standard equipment on every model. The Lord did a good thing for us men when he made them like this, *provided* we understand how it works and work it right. How it goes here is that a woman finds it very difficult to accept unfaithfulness in any form. But, thank goodness, the reverse is also true. She can't help loving more and more a man she knows is utterly dependable. Because this is so, early in your marriage you should look her squarely in the eye and solemnly swear:

"Neither by day or by night will I ever cut you down in company. Not before my family, your family, our family. Not before friends, acquaintances, strangers. When you are with me or behind your back. *Never* by wisecrack, or snide remark, or in any manner do I intend to be anything other than one hundred percent loyal!"

3. *Never compare her unfavorably with other women.*

I remember one little wife who married a widower. He was a good catch and she was glad to get him. But she got one thing she didn't like and that's why she came to see me. "What happened," she said, "was that, after we left the church, his ex-wife seemed to come alive and I'm right up to here with her. I know how she cooked, how she looked, how she walked, how she talked. In fact," she concluded, "I don't think it's going to work unless we can get him de-Helenized!"

We couldn't! I regret to report this poor man never learned that you cannot win one woman by repeated recitation of another woman's merits.

This goes for all types and every perfect creature, ex-girl friends, neighbors, other men's wives, good-looking secretaries, movie stars, that doll on the magazine cover, the one on the billboard, widows, divorcees, singles, plus your mother. They are all in it together.

One of the commonest mistakes I see on the other-woman theme is the guy who has never put his mom where she belongs. I'm glad you have such a high opinion of yours. She can cook with the best. She can also keep house. She's lots of fun and I think she's the greatest. But that's for me, not you! You have a new first loyalty now and you better be sure Marilyn knows that Marilyn is number one in your heart.

If I bear down hard on this point, it is because I have known too many men who have never been told, or else they've forgotten that you can never reshape one woman by constant comparison with another.

4. *Never drop a delayed bomb.*

These come in several types and some of them are lethal. What I have in mind here is things like this:

Suddenly telling her you don't like something she's been doing a long time. To give a woman the idea that she has been displeasing you all these years without your saying one word can be a somewhat shattering experience. If she thinks at all, she's going to be asking "What else doesn't he like?" It makes her nervous. It shakes her confidence in herself, in you, and in the future. Of course, if you just now realized that you don't like it, that's something else. But even here there is a right and wrong way to get your point across and you better be sure you learn the difference.

5. *Never go away when she is crying.*

This goes for when she's weeping inside and you know it; or when her eyes are only slightly misty; or when she cries up a river.

Whether you caused it, or somebody else, makes no difference.

Tears are a time for tenderness and there is only one move to make here. That is to draw her close and tell her you're sorry.

"For goodness sake, Marilyn, grow up!" are six more words that should never cross your lips. Maybe she needs a good cry. There is therapy sometimes in tears, and especially so for a woman if she has a big, strong shoulder to cry on. She will cherish these moments forever if you let her know that you care and you want to share them with her.

6. *Never lay a hand on her except in love.*

Of course, it's illegal in some places, but even where it isn't, rough physical treatment is likely to inflict permanent damage. Most wives can forgive their husbands for not being Valentino, for not being an intellectual heavyweight, for not being vice-president of the company—but the man who resorts to brute force is something else.

One thing he is for sure is a disgrace to the male I.Q. Remember the old Chinese proverb, "He who strikes the first blow has run out of ideas." So if you are ever tempted to let one fly, then go take the dog on a tour of the lamp posts; or suddenly remember an important engagement; or if you don't think that will give you enough time, then pack your Pepsodent and leave for a spell. Anything but a haymaker!

I have known too many husbands who struck their wives and then came with the broken pieces for putting them back together. Naturally, we do the best we can, but with some things you can never recover the old splendor. Some of these poor fools are sick, some are plain mean, and some have yet to grow up. But they are all terribly hard for me to work with. The reason, I'm sure, is partly my fault. I just happen to believe that, if all the men who would hit a woman were laid end to end, it would be a good thing.

That's enough for the "nevers." Tomorrow we'll take a look at "A Few Try Not To's."

Till then,
Dad

The Seventeenth Letter: And a Few "Try Not To's"

Dear Phil,

Yesterday we had a look at "A Half-Dozen 'Nevers,'" any one of which could fracture your marriage. Today I'd like to run through a few matters that might not break a woman's heart, but they could give her the bends enough to affect your relationship negatively.

These are what I call my "try not to's." I pass them along in the same spirit as all these letters. Here are some husband thoughts that have been helpful at our house. In reporting them I hope you'll take what seems worthwhile into your own mind and come up with things even better for your life with Marilyn.

Remember that treating a woman right is like putting money in the bank. One day you'll be glad you did. My experience would indicate that if you make regular deposits during the early years, the years following will pay back dividends many times over. I have also observed enough real oldies close up to believe that a good union, rightly put together over the first half, can go only one way from there—better! When your joints are ancient and creaky and you begin to dodder, there could hardly be anything finer than living in a loving relationship which you *know* you helped create. You are aware that I believe in living *today* to the fullest. But it's a smart man who lifts his eyes now and then for the long look.

Practically all of these "try not to's" require some thinking ahead. For example, here is the husband who comes home one night from work and says, "I'm going to Hawaii on business tomorrow and I thought it would be nice if you would go with me." This is bound to be great, good news, and what wife wouldn't be perfectly delirious with delight? I'll tell you what wife wouldn't! The one who finds out that her husband has known about this trip for three weeks, only he forgot to mention it.

You can see what this does to her. Whether she has children to think about (baby-sitter, food preparations, school car pool, plus numberless other things known only to mothers), or whether she has only herself to get ready (clothes to select, hairdresser to see, important committee to chair, plus numberless other things known only to women without children)—you can take it from one who learned by experience—this is no way to treat a woman. Even though she counts herself lucky to have a man who wants her along; though she knocks herself out to get ready; though she finally plops on the plane exhausted; you'll have a better time, both on this trip and the last one you take together, if you try not to treat her this way!

Of course if you've only found out today that you're leaving tomorrow, she'll make the best of it, and she can bear it partially because she knows you're in the same jam. But whether it's Hawaii, or an afternoon trip across town, or a visit upstate where she could run in on her kinfolk, or any other situation of any kind, you get the point. She'll love you more if she knows that some of your nice gestures have been well thought out with her convenience in mind.

The same applies right down to the little things, like asking her to get your best suit ready a day ahead instead of blowing your stack because it's at the cleaners when you have a crucial appointment this very morning only you forgot to say so.

Living with this absent-minded professor type must be terribly exasperating even to those saintly souls who hardly ever droop their wings. A woman is a woman, and that means she likes all the time you can give her for big deals, little deals, and all the deals in between.

Another "try not to" you'll do well to ponder is in the realm of sharing what you know which might embarrass her late if somebody knew you knew but you forgot to tell her.

For example, suppose you heard that one of your couple friends had their new baby. What if she met the proud father two days later and inquired, "How's Betty?" with nary a word of congratulations? If he knows that you know and you simply failed to pass the glad tidings along, see what you've done? You have made yourself out a first-class failure as a friend and mortified Marilyn unnecessarily. That isn't all! You've left her wondering "What else isn't he telling?" And if you repeat this faux pas regularly you leave yourself wide open for questions like "What's the matter? Aren't they speaking?" ... "Poor girl! It must be tough to live with a man that thoughtless."

So whether it's a new baby, or that Mrs. Logan's mother died, or that they discovered oil in the Adams' orchard, or that you heard the neighbors have smallpox, learn to make some little pigeon holes somewhere in your head for things like this and pass them along.

There are several other items on my list of "try not to's," but your own collection will be more valuable to you than mine. There *is* one more I probably should mention because I have heard so many women complain about this one. Those wives who must endure it tell me that it gets awfully old for their husbands *never* to notice the new things. New hairdo, new dress, new perfume, new negligee, new anything. I was recently discussing how to treat a woman in a study group on marriage and this subject came up. One woman who deserved better (she was rather attractive, I thought) made this comment: "If I came home driving a new Cadillac he might possibly see that. New Cadillacs cost money. But I'm telling you the truth, if I started wearing an eye patch, I doubt if he'd notice that for six weeks!"

Let's hope she was exaggerating to get her point across. But there is no kidding about this—the more observant you are, the better she'll like you.

Try not to forget that, too!
Dad

The Eighteenth Letter: Some Moments Are Only For Her

Dear Phil,

I'm at the office now and things have finally quieted down after one of those "woolly booger" mornings. Just talked to your mother and she sends her love.

A few letters back I referred to what I call "the embarrassing personal memoirs of yours truly." This little beaut I am about to tell you is one of these. It will take us down an important sideroad off the "people and things" theme.

What I did on this occasion was to phone your mother about midafternoon. I began with one of her favorites, like "All I wanted was to hear your voice!" or "I just saw an interesting arrangement of molecules and it made me think of you." Then we carried on from there.

Up to here, we were going great. But then, right in the middle of the flowers, I asked, "Say, has the mail come? Did we get the check from our tax return?"

Now there is nothing wrong with tax refunds. She likes them. I like them. But I had started with "*All* I wanted," remember?

So the next sound you hear is that of the great lover falling flat on his face. There was a long silence. You know how your mother is. When there is nothing to say she says nothing.

I made several attempts to get back where we'd been, but sometimes, like the Bible says, "The mouth of a fool poureth out foolishness."

It did. Having thoroughly clobbered a very nice moment, I said good-bye and did me some thinking. What I came up with was that a man can destroy some fine things by crowding. I had let my question kill my compliment.

So, it is not true that, just because you are married, anything goes. Certainly there are days when the telephone ringing—"All I wanted was to hear you"—the U.S. mail, tax refunds, and everything you're thinking, plus everything she's thinking mixes together to brighten your love.

Then there are other times when, if you're not careful, you mess the whole thing up by mixing your subjects. I wish I had the exact words to tell you how to select and distinguish. But I guess this is one of those narrow places where each must go it alone and learn for himself.

I hope you do learn it, because most women tell me it is the unimportant, over-looked items that make the difference between the great lover and just another husband. And the great ones seem to sense that *sometimes a woman likes to believe her man is concentrating exclusively on her; that he has nothing else in mind but her; that she is interesting enough to absorb him completely.*

Stay alert,
Dad

P.S. I am sure you have already concluded that if the eager beaver in me just *had* to know about that tax refund, he could have hung up and called back later.

The Nineteenth Letter: Dialogue On Moods

Dear Phil,

If you ever catch yourself saying "Women, I can't understand them!" don't forget to add "Thank God!" This is one of the things that makes marriage so much fun.

I have told you a number of places where you can depend on your wife's reactions. But another sure thing is that she will love you more if you learn how to handle her when she isn't dependable.

Psychologists tell us that the best climate for healthy growth is one in which we can express the entire range of our feelings. It should be an aim of your marriage to develop your relationship until you can each say what you feel like saying, do what you feel like doing, and be what you feel like being.

But don't hurry it. The total liberty to exercise one's numerous selves without restraint is another of those things you should put with your long-range goals. Unless you go at this right you might possibly tear up so much during the first twelve months it would take that many years to put it back together.

You can see we are talking about a very subtle business. Since every person is different from every other person, and because each one of us is also different on different days (years, months, weeks, hours, too) I decided to spread out for ideas. Toward this end I called together a half-dozen men whom I know well enough for a bull session on marriage and moods.

These fellows earn their livings in widely divergent fields and they are personally just about as varied as six men could be. But they are all alike here—they are successful husbands.

I told them why I wanted their reactions, so they knew that part of what they said would go into a letter to you. You can see that they got right down to it, and I give you their conversation (censored slightly) as it came from the tape. I have arranged what they said in general headings and added my own thoughts in parentheses.

Miscellaneous comments on the mood theme:

"My job is sales and I have to study my customers' moods. Seems to me it works better when I think of my wife as one of my customers and do the same for her."

"That's the secret right there. So many times we're smart at business and stupid at home. Sometimes it hits me hard that I treat people nice all day and act like a heel with the family."

(Do you remember the old poem of unknown authorship that I taught you long ago?) "There's one sad truth in life I've found, while journeying east to west:/The only folks we really wound are those we love the best./We flatter those we scarcely know, we please the fleeting guest,/and deal full many a thoughtless blow to those we love the best.")

"I think one of the big things is to have sort of a blow-off session with myself on the way home. Kind of a de-pressurizing thing. My wife seems to match her mood to mine. If I come home happy, she's happy. If I'm owly, she's owly."

"My wife is one hundred percent dependable—bitchy all the time! But after wrestling with the kids all day I'd be like that too. So it's up to me to spend some time getting *her* de-pressurized."

"Well at our house it's a matter of whoever is down pulling the other one up. Sometimes it's me. Sometimes her. It's kind of an unspoken agreement. We sort of test each other to see which one has the job to do."

Interesting comments on variability in women:

"One time my wife is sharp as a lady lawyer. Next time she asks me a stupid question like 'Who wrote the autobiography of Gypsy Rose Lee?' If a fellow is smart enough to know when his wife is dumb he can get by with plenty. Tell him that. Might come in handy."

"Yeah! It's all a matter of moods. Today she wants to cry. Tomorrow she wants to laugh. This week she's a lamb. Next week, get out of the way."

"Tell the kid it works like that in the bedroom too. One time your wife reminds you of that novel where the missionaries go around pushing brassieres for the natives. Next time she acts like something out of a French movie. You've got to know which mood they're in before you know which way you'd better be!"

Comments relative to the recognition of moods:

"Would you believe it? My wife's moods seem to be taken from the weather?"

"I read somewhere that you can tell a lot about a woman by studying her menstrual cycle. I believe it. There's one period when she can't do enough nice things for you. Then there's a few days when she wants you to baby her. If I remember this and play up to it things go better with us."

"I learned in medical school there actually are hormonal changes then that *do* cause moods. We had a rough time before I accepted this."

"My wife wears her moods, if you know what I mean! I can almost tell what's going on in her head by the way she dresses."

Thoughts on how to handle women in their moods:

"For my money, the secret is to allow her plenty of freedom. Like you say, togetherness of the best kind is built on the right kind of apartness. She needs to have some friends of her own. She ought to go some places I don't go. If I give her this kind of liberty she gets a lot of this mood stuff out of her system. She's also less possessive of me, which makes it nicer all around."

(What he is saying is that he gives her room to be herself so she gives him room to be himself. We've been over this road before, but it's worth a repeat. That's a great word for eventual oneness—*room!*

"Jack, you mentioned that sometimes Alice wants to baby you. The thing in our relationship is for me not to miss those times. I think the man should be head of the house, but sometimes he needs to make like an infant. It goes better with Joan if I let her mother me once in a while. This seems to get something out of her system, and besides I like it now and then myself."

"Geraldine tends to want her own way most of the time. I used to bow my neck, but then I did some thinking. There are a whole lot of places where it really doesn't matter. So I just 'yes, yes' her on all the little things. Then when something big comes along I say 'Here's how it's going to be.' It sure goes better with us when I remember to follow that rule."

"Of course we wouldn't be for making your boy a con man, but it's a sure thing there are some tricks he better learn to play."

"Let's go back to Tom's theme about freedom outside the home, different interests, and so forth. This also goes for when you're together. Sometimes one of you wants conversation. Then there are other days when all you want is privacy, silence, no intrusion."

"The main thing with Mary Jo is for me to feel bad when she feels bad. I used to say 'Snap out of it!' That was before I got smart. Tell him to bleed when she bleeds."

"You know what I do when my wife gets to feeling bad? If I can get her in the car I drive her through the slums. Seems like seeing all those things and then coming home brings her out of it."

"Me? I take Geraldine to a comedy!"

"Works just the opposite for us. If I can find a real sad movie I take her there. Guess she gets it out of her system through other people's sadness. What do they call it? Vicarious?"

"One thing that can throw Alice into a tailspin quicker than anything is to make fun of some crazy thing she wants to do. If it's too far out of course I've got to do something, but most of the time it's better to let her go ahead. The way I got it figured is that she'll be happier if she finds out for herself that it won't work. Or how do I know, she may need to fail for her own good. Then there was this time I was sure she'd flipped and darned if she didn't come up with a brilliant idea."

"You should have certain little jokes between you that can always bring a laugh. Sometimes when you see her headed for a bad mood if you can get her laughing you can break it up."

"Any of you fellows have trouble with jealousy? That's a bad mood he better learn to handle. When we were first married I tried everything. Teasing, closing myself off, really giving her something to be jealous about! I even went to a psychiatrist. He told me I should remember she wasn't afraid of what the other woman had, but afraid of what she didn't have. He said if I would build her up with big doses of assurance this would cure it. So that's what I've been doing and it really works!"

Interesting observations, aren't they? As I said at the outset, these are all unusually good husbands. Maybe I should tell you who they are: a salesman, a vice-president of a major oil company, a postal employee, a professor of creative writing, a rancher, and a medical student majoring in psychiatry. Yet they all have this one thing in common—their wives think they are the greatest!

Yours will too if you learn how to handle her moods.

Have fun,
Dad

The Twentieth Letter: Troubles Are for Sharing

Dear Phil,

Doc Wilkinson gave me an important lesson about how to treat a woman. What he did was to convince me that a man better learn to share his problems with his wife at the right time—and totally.

We were riding together that night to see a lady who had frantically phoned both of us—her doctor *and* her minister. This gal wanted to be good and ready. She claimed that she was "about to depart this vale of tears." (Her words.)

I was a young pastor fresh out of seminary. Doc had stopped to pick me up, as he was often to do later because we became the best of friends.

I wish you could have known him. He had a face like the old oaken bucket, but his heart was beautiful. To my knowledge he never turned anyone down who needed help; it would probably have taken a computer to total what people owed him in unpaid accounts; and when he died it was like a familiar old tree going down outside your window. He loved people and he could read right through them. He was one of the greatest teachers of "country psychology" I have known.

He was reading me that night. I was nervous as a green rookie up to bat for the first time in spring training. "Relax preacher," he drawled. Then in his slow, deep voice he went on, "She's not going to die. We'll fix her up, you and me together. Oh I don't mean she's got no troubles. She's got plenty, but they're all imaginary."

Then he went on to spin her story. Her husband had died the year before, and Doc summed that up like this: "Though I don't like to speak disrespectful of the dead, he really ruined her."

Seems that Henry was a good man, but "he babied her something awful." Once the cholera wiped out his herd, but he never told her. If his feeders lost money he kept that from her too. The year the barn burned Doc allowed she would never have known that either except she could see it going up in smoke.

"It's a real mistake to do a woman like that," Doc contended. "Sooner or later she'll dream up allergies and headaches and even female trouble just to give her mind something to do. A woman needs drama, that's what, and if she don't get it where she should she'll get it where she shouldn't."

The years since I heard him say this have proven how right he was. I have actually seen women take to their beds for what looked like assurance that their lives really mattered. In several of these cases my mind went back to Doc Wilkinson's lesson, and, sure enough, there was an overprotective husband trying to be a hero.

The reason why I wanted you to have this letter is that I hear too many men saying "But I don't want to concern her with my problems. After all, she has enough to worry about." (They usually say this as if they were expecting some kind of medal.)

If you ever catch yourself at this or anything like it, I hope you'll do a retake. You stood one day with Marilyn and promised to share your life "in plenty *and* in want, in joy *and* in sorrow." The husband who forgets this may be in for more trouble tomorrow than he would have today if he simply opened up and gave it to her straight.

Of course there are right and wrong ways to let our sorrows be known and there will be times when a brief postponement may be in order. But the rule has got to be that troubles are for sharing, and you deny your wife a lot if you don't believe it.

For one thing, you have cut her out of that sense of partnership, which is among the deeper reasons for marriage. "Together" is one of the most beautiful words in our vocabulary and it takes on special beauty when it indicates that two people are closing the gaps between them by drawing shoulder to shoulder against all comers.

Then, too, you insult her intelligence when you don't let her help you think your troubles through. Being as smart as Marilyn is she is very likely to sense that something is bothering you. If she has to dig this out of you time after time, sooner or later she's going to be bothered with a bunch of questions coming from that place in a woman's heart where questions congregate.

"What's the matter with *me*? Doesn't he trust me?" ... "Does he think I'm not wise enough to help him figure things out?" ... "Is there someone else he's telling his troubles to?" ... And so on to a real tizzy.

We both know that there are some women whose intelligence quotient is not exactly overwhelming. But if we were to trace their lack of wisdom back to its origin, we might find it was not that they were innately lacking. They were never given a chance to develop what they had.

Yet even where there is a wide gap, this can be closed by a wise husband. I have known some couples where he was brilliant and, to borrow one of your own phrases, "she didn't know from nothin'." But he found help from thinking out loud in her presence and she felt honored to be his listening post.

If you are smart in areas she isn't she may be all the more thrilled if you take her into your confidence. She'll tuck these happy moments in a corner of her mind for later reference—"Just think, my clever, gifted husband asked *me* what I thought!"

There is one further wrong you do her if you refrain from sharing your troubles at the right time in the right way. If you come through your difficulties with banners flying and tell her about it afterward you have denied her the thrill of participation in success. Of course it's nice when friends hit it big on their own. Three cheers for them! But there is a special glow in the celebration if we feel that we made even a small contribution to their success.

So put it all together and what does it say? It says what Doc said, "It's a real mistake to do a woman like that." Strange as it may seem, in the long run sharing your unhappiness with your wife is one way to keep her happy.

"Bear ye one another's burdens,"

Dad

The Twenty-first Letter: Fight the Good Fight

Dear Phil,

In one town where I lived two rivers met. There was a bluff high above them where you could sit and watch their coming together. It was a wonderful place for lovers to park and study miscellaneous matters of communication.

I am not thinking right now what you think I am thinking. What I am wishing is that I could take you and Marilyn there and then leave you to watch those two rivers in their meeting.

You would observe that well upstream, before they united, each river flowed gently along. But right at the point of their union, look out!

Those two nice streams came at each other like fury. I have actually seen them on days when it was almost frightening to watch. They clashed in a wild commotion of frenzy and confusion. They hurled themselves head on as if each was determined that the other should end its existence right there.

Then, as you watched, you could almost see the angry white caps pair off, bow in respect to each other, and join forces as if to say "Let us get along now. Ahead of us there is something better."

Sure enough, on downstream, at some distance, the river swept steadily on once more. It was broader there, more majestic, and it gave you the feeling that something good had been fashioned out of the conflict.

A good marriage is often like that. When two independent streams of existence come together, there will probably be some dashing of life against life at the juncture. Personalities rush against each other. Preferences clash. Ideas contend for power and habits vie for position. Sometimes, like the waves, they throw up a spray that leaves you breathless and makes you wonder where has the loveliness gone.

But that's all right. Like the two rivers, what comes out of their struggle may be something deeper, more powerful than what they were on their own.

So the first thing you and Marilyn should do about hostility is to *accept it as a natural part of life for two red-blooded young people building a home together.* Many newlyweds panic at the first indication that there may be things somebody doesn't like around here. One young bride put it like this when she wrote to describe their first quarrel. "I guess we expected the last verse of 'How Many Ways Do I Love Thee' to go on singing itself forever."

It won't. The truth is that life would be somewhat dull if it did. No small part of the zest in a good marriage comes from working through differences. Learning to zig and zag with the entanglements; studying each other's emotions intelligently; all these offer a challenge that simply can't be beat for sheer fun and excitement.

The rule you grew up under at home was "Never be ashamed of anger. It is a natural part of being a useful person. The only thing you need to regret is when you handle it badly." If I were you, I would pass that bit of philosophy along to Marilyn and make it part of your thinking together. It will be a blessing to your marriage and make you both healthier. Ulcers come from repressed ill will. So do allergies, headaches, high blood pressure, moods, nagging, infidelity, divorce, and a lot of other things you can do without.

The second thing you should do about hostility is to *work up some kind of covenant under which you will agree to settle your differences.*

You will remember that in *Letters to Karen* I set down what your mother and I call "Our Seven Official Rules for a Good,

Clean Fight." We decided to make these public not because they are the last word, but because they have done so much for us. I am repeating them here with a few comments for your consideration.

1. **Before we begin we must both agree that the time is right.** The Bible warns that we are foolish to say "peace, peace, when there is no peace." But it also offers us this beautiful prayer: "Set a watch before my lips. Keep the door of my mouth." I have found that an excellent petition. There are days when all she wants is tender, loving care. Then there are other times when the light of battle leaps to her eyes and you can sense that she is ready. So, unless you are totally exhausted yourself, push on back to where she has bivouacked her troops and sound the battle cry. Let her know that you love her and if what your love needs right now is war, you're ready too.

2. **We will remember that our only aim is deeper understanding.** One sure test for maturity is the ability to react with sympathy toward hostility sent our way. This obviously is no small accomplishment, but it should be a personal goal toward which you move at a steady pace. When some brickbat hits, our normal reaction is to look for something to throw back. But the great husband disciplines himself to say "Maybe she's got a problem! How can I help her?" You can do this partially by remembering that most anger is the result of a whole lot which has gone before. Sometimes her rage has such a long history that you actually had very little to do with it. In this sense she's not angry at you as much as she is at those whom you've recalled by whatever it is you've done. So, never ask yourself how some innocent little remark, or some insignificant act, could cause such furor. This was only the match that lit the keg where she's been stashing her frustration. What she needs now is ventilation. The big man even learns to postpone his defense until his woman has thoroughly rid

herself of whatever it is that's bugging her. Some moments aren't for explanation, but for listening. One of these is when she's only half through.

3. **We will check our weapons often to be sure they're not deadly.** Have you noticed the nuclear war tacticians using the interesting term "over-kill"? What they are talking about is slaughtering more than necessary to win the war. I think that sounds an important warning for the handling of conflict at home. One thing you sure don't want to destroy is her pride. When a woman's pride is damaged, her sense of values gets warped and that lets loose a cage full of monsters. You will avoid this serious error if you *aim to attack the problem, not the person!* Any conflict between you should leave you both intact at heart. Keep always before you the thought that you're not fighting to obliterate each other. This isn't Antietam or some other struggle to death. Then make it your aim to hold the battle fires to just the right intensity. If you do this with skill, the heat you generate may serve to warm your marriage later to a very nice temperature.

4. **We will lower our voices one notch instead of raising them two.** One of the nicest things your mother taught me was that we could get the job done as well by whispering it through rather than shouting it down.

Try this just once and I think you'll like it. Obviously, this calls for considerable discipline, but you can bet it's worth the effort. Pulverizing each other with words can be good. Getting it all out is also important. But you better learn some neuter nouns, a few sterile adjectives, and certain phrases that can be interpreted several ways. The tone of your voice, and especially the volume, is something else. The tendency is for the sound to go higher and higher with the mounting ire. So, if you've got what it takes to do this, live by the agreement that you will say it softly as you say it thoroughly.

5. **We will never quarrel or reveal private matters in public.** We've been over this road before, but let's note another thing in passing. It's a good idea when you're quarreling to stay away from your main source of sympathy outside the home. Your best friend, fishing partner, somebody at the office, or your mother may build up your ego and assure you that anyone as fine as you just has to be one hundred percent in the clear. But there are two things wrong with running this way when you're wounded: (a) every time you tell it, you probably make it a little bit worse than it really is; (b) going to them keeps you from going to the one person you'll finally have to settle it with, namely, Marilyn!

6. **We will discuss an armistice whenever either of us calls "halt."** This, too, requires a delicate sense of judgment. If she waves even a drooping olive branch, you'd better open your arms and welcome her there. Because each person is different and every combination of individuals is unique, you must learn by trial and error your own fine line of "enough" and "too much." One couple I know does a clever thing. They have what they call "The Committee!" This is not some outside influence. It is rather their pre-agreed signal that whenever one of them says "I think we should refer it now to The Committee," this is their moment for "cease-fire."

7. **When we have come to terms, we will put it away till we both agree it needs more discussing.** This is especially important for newlyweds. Many young couples I know operate under the delusion that *everything* has to be settled this very day. There is one thing wrong with that—it isn't so! Some questions can fall to the floor unanswered and you can still love to the maximum even if there are matters you intend to take up later for further consideration. Point to remember: *Don't try to force more unanimity than your marriage is prepared to handle at any given stage of your development!* A great husband-wife relationship does not mean

that these two have reached the peak of human coalescing. It more likely indicates that they are living up to their capacity for oneness this day with the understanding that tomorrow will give them more capacity for more total togetherness.

We have said that to fight the good fight...

HOLD EVERYTHING! Mark Abadie just fell out of his tree house and we've got to go to the hospital. If I don't make it back here today, I'll give you a rundown tomorrow.

Same evening: Here I am back at my typewriter after a rush trip to St. Lukes. The poor kid broke both heels, several ribs, and one elbow. He's really hurting.

Just last week your mother and I were sitting on our love seat watching Mark shinny up the tree and then swing by the rope straight over to the doorway. It's a scary sight, but he makes it look easy. Every time I see him, though, I say a prayer of thanks that we got you raised with no major accidents. I have yet to see the tree you couldn't climb and you could never make me believe there aren't special angels assigned to little boys. Come to think of it, I guess Mark has one too. He might have landed on his head when the rope broke and thirty-five feet is no small fall. So, like most such times, there are some things to be glad about. Being a man, I'm sure you'll understand when I say one thing I'm glad about is that it wasn't our tree house. That one must have a whole bunch of special angels.

Well, that's a long digression, but knowing you have a large measure of sympathy, I knew you'd want to be thinking of Mark. Timmy will give you a fuller account, and since he got in here, that makes another thing I'm thankful for. At nine he's already too heavy to climb many more feet up than he is years old.

But we better get back to our business. I was saying that to fight the good fight...you must accept hostility as a natural part of life and you will need some rules for surfacing things you don't like.

There is another all-important consideration in fighting the good fight. This is the *offering of apologies, the request for forgiveness, and the assurance that you will do your best to forget.*

These things are especially important for husbands because the words "I'm sorry" and the language of forgiveness seem more difficult for men than women. One poor wife told me recently, "My husband's idea of settling a quarrel is to put me in his sweat box until I say, 'You were *all* right! It was my fault *completely!'* The truth is," she went on, "I've just about had it! He thinks that he and God are the only perfect beings and he may even have some questions about God!"

So help me, that's what the lady said. Marriage for her is an excruciating experience. One mark of pure hell is the absence of mercy, and for this particular gal, life has become pure hell.

Remember then that the measurement of bigness in a man is never taken at the point of a bowed neck. It is rather determined from the spot where he can unbend in true humility to pay his honest debts with these five words: "I was wrong. Forgive me."

But suppose it was *all* her fault. She really did it this time. Now what will you do? One thing you can do is to give her an opening. How about saying "I'm sorry we're having trouble. I don't like it this way. Let's stick together, what do you say?" What she will probably say is "Well, I *was* a little bit foolish myself." A woman never forgets things like this. You have opened the gate where she can come through to set the matter straight. She'll love you forever for that.

This movement-to-get-things-settled is always much more important than who started it. Tell yourself that pointing up the origin doesn't matter nearly as much as how to make things right once more. If you keep this goal before you, the day will come when you'll be stumbling over each other as though there were a prize for the person who got there first to restore the relationship.

Another test of how mature you both are is your ability to forget what you've forgiven. Or, if the offense was one of those devastating things no normal person could possibly forget, then can you put it where it belongs? Even better, can you work it into the fabric of your love to make your marriage more of a blessing to you both? You can see that to be a good husband you must work at never forgetting some things while you work at never remembering others.

Love, after a quarrel, can be a greater thing than it was before no matter who scored the most points or who brought it on. This is a law of life. All up and down the line that's how it goes. History makes it plain that people who have fought each other in one generation turn out to be the strongest allies in the next. Why? Of course it is partially because we need them and they need us now. But there is more to it than that.

After the smoke is cleared and the truce is signed, we find that all the time they are really very much like we are. They dream the same dreams, hope the same hopes, struggle just like we struggle. We learn to admire their abilities and the things we didn't know when we were fighting actually thrill us now. Always when people get rid of rancor, love comes to its place. It opens up vast ranges for sympathy and understanding and a genuine desire to know more of what's going on.

I have a feeling that our future existence as a human race depends on this: *Can we learn methods of clearing the hostility so that we make room for the love which is always moving in?*

Do you believe the time is coming when the nations will live together in permanent peace? That will be the day, won't it? Well, it sure can't start unless it starts somewhere.

It is some goal for any couple to see their marriage as a contribution to that.

Dad

The Twenty-second Letter: Rural Wisdom

Dear Phil,

This is one of those days when things are jumping up and down for doing. I was about to check it off as no time for letter writing when I recalled a quaint saying about that "over-kill" theme we considered.

What it says is:

"Never burn down the house to get rid of your mice"

I think this says something worth pondering on the hostility theme. So do several others I found as I rummaged through my country proverb file to check the exact wording on this one.

So I'll pass these along as today's contribution to your thoughts on how to treat a woman. Knowing you, I'm sure they will turn up their own lessons as you think them through.

"Only a fool spits into the wind"

"Never throw stones at a cat on a greenhouse"

"Always stand behind a gun and in front of a mule"

"Never put your wishbone where your backbone ought to be"

Whimsically,
Dad

The Twenty-third Letter: Money Maxims

Dear Phil,

Any survey of marital problems will include money high on the list of trouble causers. There are several reasons why this is true. For one thing, every husband-wife combination brings to the marriage different concepts. One may have been brought up by parents who indulged every want. The other may be tied up inside with a poverty complex. This person might have been raised on the installment plan. Perhaps the other heard over and over "Strictly cash! Save first, then buy!" There are dozens of other differences out of your backgrounds that may need to be analyzed.

So, early in your marriage you should consider why you each think like you do and work out a philosophy for the future that you can both live with. A basic thought structure can undergird your family financially and help to secure your marriage.

Toward this end, I present here three money maxims that your mother and I have developed through the years.

Maxim 1: *Attitude counts more than amount!*

The question is not how much you have or don't have. What matters most is how you look at it. I have known some people who were financially loaded—yet they were inwardly miserable. I have known others who had very little—yet there was a song in their hearts.

Make up your mind that you're not going to be personally happy until you get control of your money. Note I didn't say "get money" but "get control." There is one whale of a difference. Getting control doesn't mean sitting like a watchdog guarding expenditures. Neither is it a matter of having big chunks to total up or to invest at six percent. What counts is that you take charge mentally of what you do have rather than vice versa. A whole lot of folks let their money manage them, direct their thinking and rule their hearts.

Some anonymous country poet puts it like this:

> It's not how well I'd be doing
> If a million should fall to my lot;
> But what am I thinking today
> About the dollar and a quarter I've got!

Maxim 2: *Live today before tomorrow!*

This one we adopted because so many people we know are operating with a delusion. They think that when they get more dollars then they will enjoy life.

I hear this often in the consultation room: "When we get the house paid for ... the kids through college ... a little bit more in our savings ... one more promotion ... when business doubles ... and we can carpet the living room ... or build our own swimming pool ... or buy that summer house we've dreamed about ... or afford fine clothes ... or join the better clubs ... that will be really living!"

In one sense it is easy to see why so many people fall into this trap. Every media of communication is harnessed to make us want what we don't have and be dissatisfied until we get more things. With all the gusto of an old-time evangelist, the announcer dins in our ears that we will never arrive until we drive this sports car or fly this luxury airliner to somewhere. "Be nice to number one!" "Give yourself a treat!" "You owe it to your family!" Thus the gimme' guys blather on, and before we know it we're hooked.

Of course, it's fun to look forward. Anticipation adds zest. I hope you'll adopt a savings plan and keep some goals out there ahead of you. But don't let your dreams of tomorrow sweep today and all of its pleasures off to one side.

Here are some great words for young couples from the Bible: "*This* is the day which the Lord hath made. We will rejoice and be glad in it!"

Maxim 3: *Outgo affects income!*

Sounds crazy, doesn't it, to say that one way to have more is to give more? But this is how we've found it in our marriage. With no exception, every time we increased our giving to help others beyond our own doors, some blessing followed that we hadn't expected. It has happened so often we have come to this conclusion: *The secret to family finance is to quit worrying so much about the intake and open up the outlets until they are what they ought to be.*

As you know, we have operated our family budget on this policy: "Give ten percent, save ten percent, and spend the rest with thanksgiving and praise!"

Of course it isn't true that everybody who tithes gets rich, and it isn't so that all who get rich are good givers. But it is a fact that life for us is only what it ought to be when our giving is what it ought to be.

So, if I were you, I would establish some rule of life early in your marriage and grow in your sense of stewardship. When you see your money as a means of helping others, or for helping God help others, you have: (a) protected yourselves from the miseries of selfishness; (b) built in a guard against losing your bearings as you prosper; (c) put yourself in a position to experience one of life's greatest thrills—that of knowing many blessings because you are a blessing to many.

You are sharp enough to observe that giving in order to get is not what this is about. But getting in order to give touches the very core of life's meaning. Those who will dare to launch out at this point will find that the God of abundance is looking for places through which he can pour his riches to bless others. At the heart of his universe, he has written certain laws, and one of these is that love comes back to the lover, joy returns to the giver, and contentment at its fullest is for those whose accounts are right.

Happy spending,
Dad

The Twenty-fourth Letter: Clothes, Hair, and Miscellany

Dear Phil,

In my last letter I told you certain principles your mother and I discovered together about money. Here are some thoughts on what you as a husband can do with a few dollars to give your wife that "lucky me" feeling, which makes things nice for both of you.

Let's start with *clothes.* Whatever you can allow in your budget for Marilyn's mentionables and otherwise will bring excellent returns on the investment. Every good woman goes for nice things to wear. She likes skirts, sweaters, slacks, shorts, smocks, frocks, dresses, gowns, robes, coat (winter, spring, petti-, house, rain—these are all coats), pajamas, scarves, wraps, shawls, shoes, slippers, sandals, pumps, bonnets, caps, hats, formals, informals, and so on indefinitely. She likes all these plus a lot of additional items to go on these, with these, over and under.

Some men see all this as a threat to the family exchequer. Others make friends with the whole business and use the facts to cozy up the relationship and make their marriage merrier.

There are certain "how to's" and some "how not to's" you'd better learn and remember. One is that every woman is different. Some prefer to shop alone, and if this is how it is, you see that she has time for it and send her off with a humming heart. Let her know she has full freedom to decide for herself what she likes. And when she returns, you find something nice to say about it. Even if it's downright ludicrous, you can begin with "Well, now, that *is* a hat! I can hardly wait to see you in it!" (Be sure it isn't a handbag.)

In other words, check what you are about to say long enough to be sure it will sound like you want it to sound. How you want it to sound is a bit like the Liberty Bell. You also want your words to carry the message that you believe in her even if you aren't exactly taken with her latest purchase.

Think man! You can find something to praise. If it really is awful, maybe it was a bargain and you can praise that. Women go nuts at the bargain counter, and if you don't think so keep your eyes open and you'll see. You'll also see that she responds well if you tell her she's the best bird dog you ever saw, praise her ingenuity, and pat her on the back for saving your money.

If you do give her the wherewithal to buy by herself, go by herself, choose by herself—if you give all this and a spirit that says "If you like it, I'll like it," you have done a great thing. You have let her know that you know togetherness is never compressed. You also build yourself up in her eyes. A lot of her friends don't have husbands with hearts that generous, and aren't you the nice one?

Then there are other women who like for you to shop with them. Some prefer your company on every buying occasion and others part of the time. If she's one of these for heaven's sake go willingly and not like a sheep to the slaughter. There is, incidentally, one short line I'd never forget for these forays. It's for those moments when she steps out of the dressing room and you can tell she's wondering. If you *don't* like it and you are loath to see your earnings go for things like this, now is the time to say "I don't think it does you justice!" (Here we are once more at the same old rule: It isn't always what you do, it's how you do it that counts!)

It would seem that this is enough on clothes, but there is yet a bit of miscellany which might come in handy. One such is to always notice what she's wearing. Come on now, just one small thing like style, fit, color. It never ceases to amaze me how come men can remember the color of both teams' uniforms, or the color of every car in the block, or what color lipstick some new glamour doll wore at last month's office party, yet this same brilliant dullard couldn't possibly tell you the color of his wife's latest purchase or what she had on last night.

And speaking of what she wears when you go out, remember another thing. If she asks you beforehand what to wear, it's all right for you to tell her, but if she has spent thirty minutes getting it on and then she asks you, here's one more time to cogitate before you speculate.

Another miscellany is actually one of the "nevers." This is that you must *never* tell her you never did like that dress she's been wearing for months (hats, shoes, blouses, coats, hairdos—same thing!) "I always did think it was awful" constitutes one of the poorest arrangements of words you could possibly put together from a woman's standpoint. There is only one way the female mind can work if you do this. She pictures herself practically naked every time she's worn this outfit you never did like. That kind of feeling is enough to give any woman the vapors. So, if you really can't stand it any longer, then go buy something new or take her shopping this week and tell her anyone as lovely as she is needs a few more things for her wardrobe.

That should be enough on this except for a tip of the hat to those small items you pick up now and then as happy surprises. It is well to learn her sizes. Carry them in your wallet or in your head, and when you see something that has her name on it, buy it.

She'll love you for all these unnecessaries. Even more important, she'll love you. The cute little womanly trill "Oh, you didn't *have* to" is a whole lot cuter than you think. What it means is that she feels she's somebody special because you did something special and *you didn't have to!*

Now, let's hear about *hair.* It may seem odd to include this, too, in our thoughts on money, but this is where it belongs. Most women are trained from infancy to take great pride in their hair. They have spent hours combing it, brushing it, rolling it, rearranging it, and many other things we'd call "fussing" over it.

If you don't think hair means something special to women, the next time you drive across town and stop at the lights you notice how many women (particularly those driving alone) pat their hair, twist their hair, fondle their hair, and look at their hair in the rearview mirror.

My psychiatrist friends tell me this goes back to the mother-attention syndrome, whatever that means. I'm not really sure what it means, but one thing it means is that you can do great things for your life together if you: (a) notice it; (b) praise it; (c) allow her enough money to do with it whatever it is that women do at the beauty parlor.

I'm not sure about that either, except that there must be a lot of things going on in there besides hair. News, gossip, the latest on the latest is certainly one item that comes free with the washing and rinsing and drying and setting. But there's another extra they don't get elsewhere. This is the warm sensation a woman feels in her heart about a man who earns enough and cares enough and loves her enough to provide her this blessing.

Take it from me, it is a blessing. How do I know? I know because I have seen your mother go off to the beauty shop worn down, nerves on edge, beat, only to return restored and radiant.

Perhaps right now you can afford this only monthly. All right—she'll look forward to that with high anticipation. But when you can, push it up to twice a month and, finally, weekly; and, whatever you do, don't muff this line. If *she* has to suggest it, you've lost it forever. If *you* remind her that you're in charge around here and she deserves it, and you insist, she'll sit there basking under the heat waves singing a hymn inside for a man so delightfully domineering. You do it and you'll see what I mean. The hairdresser is a husband's best friend!

Now here again say something when she comes home. Of course if you think it looks like a bird's nest that's another thing. But don't be too hasty. Maybe something within her is struggling for expression. Perhaps this week she's trying to impress one of her lady friends. If you look long enough, you can find some good words to say about it. Perhaps she'll frighten off salesmen or turn down some amorous neighbor, or something! The main thing is not to commit the prize blunder. This is to ignore it! Nothing gives a woman the sensation of falling from great heights quite like getting all refurbished, and then the man she lives with doesn't even notice!

There is another bit of miscellany worth mentioning on this theme. For example, you can tell a lot about some women by the way they do their hair. Changes may indicate something. They might even tell you things she's thinking that she doesn't know she's thinking but you should. I'd give it a bit of study.

Then you ought to ponder how you handle her hair. Sometimes she likes you to fondle it, sometimes to pat it, sometimes to muss it. But sometimes she wants you to leave it alone, like when she's just come from the beauty shop. Only she never wants you to overlook it, ever!

Before we close this down, there are a few other things about women and men and money that might well be added. We've already discussed giving and saving and enjoying. I have purposely said little about managing.

Different couples need different ways to keep books, draw up budgets, handle book accounts, and allow for expenditures. The main thing is to have some agreement. At the outset, you may need to know to the penny what comes in, what goes out, and whatever it takes to see where it all went. Perhaps who'll do the bookwork is a matter of ego for you. You earn it, by golly, so you have the right! Later on, you may want to work out some arrangement by which she manages her part, you manage your part, and another part you manage together. Then, perhaps, when your id has had the full treatment, you'll prefer to say "Honey, you take over the books, will you? I have so many important things to do!"

But however you do it, be sure you do it fairly! I couldn't tell you the number of women I've listened to who complained about their husband's double money standard. Here a few quotes I remember:

"He buys a twenty-dollar putter and has a fit if I spend two dollars for bath oil." ... "I bought a new dress the other day and you'd have thought it was an Italian original. He really raised cain. Of course it's all right if he buys the best tailored suits. Those he needs for business." ... "He complains that I'm getting dutchy, but he won't give me one thin dime to correct the situation." ... "Before we married, he said he believed in 'share and share alike.' Then I found out what he meant. You know, like the famous horse and rabbit sausage—one horse and one rabbit!"

All this may sound a bit overdone and it probably is. But that's another thing we learn. Exaggerations usually mean that problems have been stretched way out of proportion to the way things should be. And how they should be is *fair!*

This is interesting. I was trying to think of one exception to the rule of fairness. I've known many a woman who left her man because he spent too much, drank too much, gambled too much, or even saved too much. *But I have never known one woman who left because they were poor, if he was fair when they did have it, or if she thought he would be when they got it.*

Which says what? Which says that a woman loves a man she can count on. I hope yours can count on you to be fair, to be thoughtful, to be generous, and to be smart. What that last means is that a wise husband learns to draw his wife closer by the way he handles his dollars to handle her right.

Think, man, think!
Dad

The Twenty-fifth Letter: In-laws

Dear Phil,

Some wag comes up with this whimsical observation: *"Behind every successful young husband there stands a surprised mother-in-law!"*

I like that because it has such an interesting twist halfway through the saying. But the fact is that in consultation I see this problem a whole lot less than I hear jokes about it. Maybe I've been lucky. Or perhaps I've been blinded by a mother-in-law relationship that is one of the bright lights of my own life.

Your grandmother, being one of the Lord's wise women, has thanked me a thousand times for taking her daughter to love, and each time she does it I determine that much more to love her daughter more. The truth is that, if you can win your mother-in-law over to your side, she'll give you a whole lot more credit than you deserve. There is an old line that goes, "From a man she creates a god," and one place it applies is right here.

There are a couple of reasons why she does this. For one thing, when you have children of your own you'll learn that nobody stands higher with you than those who are nice to your children. So, if you're good to her daughter, you'll warm her heart every time she thinks in the direction of your house, which, for most parents, is a whole lot.

Then there is another reason why you'll have this automatic halo working for you if you are an effective husband. Every time she recites the latest about how well you two are getting along, she is simply reaffirming the fact that her daughter is a very smart girl to have chosen so well from all those suitors. And where did she get her smart? Well, everyone knows we first learn to think under our parents' influence.

So you see you have a whole lot going for you if you can get things started right. I can't tell you all the ways to do this because every situation calls for different treatment. But you won't go far wrong if you take every opportunity to tell your in-laws how much you appreciate their daughter; how thankful you are for the great job they did; you know you are reaping the benefits of their good work, etc. Believe me, parents love those who love their own, and they can't help reacting positively to this.

Sure, there may be times when the ice is somewhat thin and you had better walk circumspectly. But when that happens, keep your brains turning over, your heart sending out all the love you can manage, your mind still grateful, *and your mouth shut.*

Like I said, I am really somewhat handicapped here due to my own good fortune and because most of the in-law problems I've seen close up have been of a different type. The sticky ones I've gotten into involved how *his* mother felt about her daughter-in-law. Some of these have been downright brutal and their gory details would add very little to how anyone, male or female, should behave themselves in any relationship.

Except for these things about getting off on the right foot, I've just about shot my wad on this subject. Only, I do have one thing in my files I'd like to pass along before I sign off. It is a letter from one who knew the problem firsthand and worked it through to a good conclusion. In part, the letter reads:

> In-laws are people, only they are people who have had the advantage of being close to the one you love before you came along. Right off the bat that could place you in an unpopular spot with them and vice versa.
>
> Looking back over some of my own experiences, I would say that since in-laws are people, they should be treated as you treat other people. If you just can't tolerate them, you can be as courteous as possible when you are forced to be with them. This ought not to be impossible. If you work with people you don't like, you usually manage to tolerate them. Perhaps it might help to think of them that way while you pray for a breakthrough.
>
> Another thing I would do is try never to initiate the negative. If they really are impossible, your mate will probably bring that up often enough to assure you that you might be thinking straight if you don't like them. In your early days together, chances are good that a few "Yes, dears" are about all that will be needed from your side. One of the main requirements is sympathy. There should be sympathy for your mate who has suffered a whole lot longer than you have with this kind of people. Then there should also be that kind of sympathy which recognizes that ugly people have ugly problems causing them

to do what they do. You might get some help if you think how tough it must be to feel like they feel. Another big need is the kind of inner honesty which faces the fact that nobody likes everybody. Maybe you wouldn't like you either if you thought like they did. And if you don't like them, there's a whole lot less turmoil inside you if you take it philosophically and determine you will not be a hypocrite. The hypocrisy that pretends too much finally becomes a terrible burden. It eventually does you in because it has a million tendons reaching out to every corner of your heart. If you let their nastiness and your dishonesty about it grow underground without ever exposing it to the light, it finally destroys your peace and ends in self-hatred.

If a husband and wife can learn to share these things together at the right time in a nice way, they can usually work out some mutual means of helping each other. If they will do this, then all the people who would divide them and all the things that pull others apart can actually work the other way.

Great thinking there, isn't it? Keep still when you should, speak up when you have to, and determine together that you will make all family problems make your love stronger.

Yours for being and having good in-laws,
Dad

The Twenty-sixth Letter: Sex—The Twenty-Year Warmup

Dear Phil,

What I want you to see in this letter is that it takes a long time to bring a woman to her full glory sexually. The trouble with so many men is that they expect sex to be "out of this world" immediately. But sex at its greatest is something you create by careful attention as the years pass. That is why I offer you now some thoughts on how to treat a woman for maximum sex at the end of your first two decades together.

Let's begin with the all-important fact that *your woman will respond to your manliness more if you never forget that she is a woman.* In other words, you must educate yourself in the difference between the sexes.

A good starting place is to remember that female responses are generally much slower than male. Let's get specific. If you are a normal husband you will be thinking about sex a great deal more than your wife. For instance, you are reading this story in which the author uses some bedroom scene to convey his message. Immediately you begin living with the characters. Marilyn, reading the same description thinks "How nice!" or "How repulsive!" or "I wonder who will inherit Aunt Phoebe's millions?"

The same thing applies to pictures. Those gorgeous nudes and near-nudes all over the place these days may drive us wild with desire. All the while our mate, reacting like a true woman, might be thinking "Such a ridiculous hairdo!"

Ditto for what we see in the flesh. Following an afternoon at the beach we may be in a frenzy to climb into bed. What is she feeling? She may be musing "I hope I didn't get too sunburned" or "That was a fine new recipe for fried chicken" or "Didn't the children have fun?"

It isn't that sex is less important to her. In fact, the paradox is that it may be more so. We see it as a momentary blast, a great, exciting release. For her it's an all-inclusive relationship that takes in much more than what happens in the act itself.

In one sense everything we have been saying in our previous letters represents sex for a woman: kindness, compliments, the fragments of devotion, how you treat her in public, whether you noticed her new blouse, that telephone call this morning, some unexpected gift you brought her, the way you treat the children, whether you let her be herself—all these are a part of her sex life! For you it may be a biological matter of the moment. For her it's more likely to be the total union of two lives culminating right now in full expression of their belonging.

In other words, if you are typically male, sex is likely to be a dominant feature of your attitude toward marriage. Sure, there are other nice things, yet all roads lead to sex. But for her, marriage is more a totality of relationships, one expression of which is the sex act. This understanding is important for your long-range thinking. Treating her right sexually is partially a matter of re-educating your mind to understand hers.

With this background it will be obvious that *two key words for your own sex training are "restraint" and "timing."*

I have a Frenchman friend who says, "eet ees better to make luf vunce a veek for seven hours zan seven times a veek for vun hour." I have always thought him somewhat addled and a bit too lady-like. Here it seems to me he is leaning to his feminine side. But what he says is worth thinking through. He is emphasizing the point that for a woman *quality* matters more than *quantity.*

Not so for you, especially during your early days as a husband. You're making up for lost time. You have a great reserve of pent-up feeling. During your early days together, and perhaps for a long time, you'll have trouble holding yourself back. But the day should come when your mind turns to *how* rather than *how often,* and that will be the day you begin moving your marriage toward long-range improvement.

Some young husbands take it as a personal insult if their wife isn't one hundred percent enthusiastic one hundred percent of the time. Part of this may have its origin in those stories we have read where every woman in the office is some kind of nympho hardly able to wait till five o'clock to burst into flames.

Whenever you read or hear things like this you will do well to cool it with a couple of facts. One is that these tales are often put together by some sex-starved male who is getting his jollies from his fantasies. Or he may be so aberrant that the only satisfaction he can experience is via his imagination. You better remember also that these come-on girls who do toss their torsos all over the place, or over-paint or under-dress, may actually be pitiful people who have no other sex life than what you see. (I will never forget that day in the barbershop when the headlines were making a great hulabaloo about this American millionaire who had married an Egyptian belly dancer. The gang was discussing, as barbershoppers are prone to do, what this was about. Whereupon the old barber droned, "If he wanted what I think he wanted he should have married some country girl from Iowa!")

Right! Sex flaunted in public is probably nothing more than that—flaunted sex! But if you hope someday to be where the action is, then take it from me—sex at its greatest is likely to be the do-it-yourself project of a thinking husband.

There are several "timing" secrets I have observed among the experts. One is that they are willing to let half pleasure go for full pleasure later. They know that in even the best marriages there will be ups and downs. Sometimes all a wife wants is to be left alone. So? So the *wise lover* learns to control his exuberance while the *fool* proceeds full steam ahead. By forcing the issue he gets what he wanted tonight. But what does that prove? To himself it may prove his virility. But what does it prove to her? If it only proves to her that he's selfish, or a bore, he hasn't gained one thing—he's lost a whole lot!

Another thing the wise husband knows is that nobody gets the same results every time. So this particular session was something less than a wow. What does he do now? He refuses to panic. He tells himself that there will still be high-voltage days and other nights to go native.

Then, too, the expert at love recognizes that a woman can enjoy sex in an entirely different way from her man. Let me share with you here something a young wife said to me in consultation. She had come for help because her husband was one of those pushers who kept insisting that there was only one manner of sex satisfaction, namely his!

What she said was, "I wish he would quit pressing me to get as excited as he does. I could enjoy it so much more if he would let me enjoy the closeness while he enjoys the excitement. Is it so wrong for me sometimes to think of sex purely as my ministry to his needs? Must I *always* feel like he feels?"

The right answer is a great big resounding "No!" Yet even some of the marriage manuals stick to the premise that a man is something less than all man unless he can bring his wife to climax every time.

In my experience as a counselor I'd have to take issue with their assumption. I know that there are numerous happy marriages where the wife, at least part of the time, gets her thrills from thrilling her husband. If you do badger your woman at this point you may drive her into a frustration that can only work one way—negative. Rule: Never let *your* neurotic needs take precedence over *her* feelings!

Freedom to express your desires is a great goal, but, for the first twenty years, remember it's more goal than reality. Sure an uninhibited sex life is what you want. But you won't get it by crushing her ideas of how it should be with your ideas of how it should be.

The eventual aim is total freedom to experiment and let yourself go. There are infinite variations in a full sex life and numberless approaches. The fact is that *nothing you do in marriage is wrong provided it doesn't hurt either member to the union physically or emotionally.* But that last word is loaded. Unless you bring her along slowly you may destroy more in one night than it would take years to recover. So the wise husband paces himself with infinite tenderness! He moves toward harmony, slowly. He knows that with some things it isn't how much or how often, but how well. Sex is one of these!

Here is another thing the good lover knows. *He is aware that he can warm his woman with words before he even lays a hand on her.*

I am not talking here about the fact that you must let each other know what you like and don't like sexually; the things you are feeling; the thoughts you are thinking. What I would like to convey is the stimulating power of language properly used as a part of good foreplay in sex.

I once asked a group of women to write down their thoughts on compliments. Some amazing things turned up. I suppose it was because they were doing this anonymously, but several included their favorite phrases of praise from the bedroom.

Out of more than fifty entries I pass along here one solid note of warning, which appeared several times, and a few sure winners.

Warning: Women resent compliments if the only ones they hear are sex gimmicks. Here are some proofs to the point:

"How can men be such unimaginative morons? The only time my husband tells me I'm nice is when he wants sex." ... "Whenever he gets rhetorical, I know what's coming." ... "He never flatters me unless we're in bed." ... "My husband has a string of what I call 'bedtime lyrics.' Just once I wish he would tell me I'm nice without an ulterior motive."

That sound you hear may be a snort from the grave of Cassanova. No expert lover would make such stupid mistakes. Tell yourself repeatedly that you must avoid anything that smacks of "using" rather than loving. The surest safeguard, obviously, is to praise her biscuits and her housekeeping; how well she manages your money; how nice she looked at the party; the new apron she made; and anything else you like about her.

Sex for a woman is one of those ultrasensitive things in which it is almost impossible to hide false motives. Therefore, if you want your sex life to rank with the best, you'd better keep checking to be sure that sincerity is a big part of the total relationship.

Now let's turn to some sure winners.

One woman wrote: "I think the little secret compliments you have together mean more to a woman than anything else. I love those intimate assurances that I have been thrilling to my husband!"

Some of the more daring entries prove that this lady thinks like a true woman.

"Sometimes when we are done making love my husband says, 'I, too, have lived!' That's my favorite." ... "One of his cutest compliments is, 'Whenever I look at you in that, it's like all my evil thoughts put together in one!'" ... "Would you believe it? Sometimes he reads me The Song of Solomon before we make love. Times like these mean everything to me."

Note how these center on a man's assurance that he is being satisfied. This is terribly important to a woman. Not only does she want to feel that she is fulfilling the basic female function of pleasing her mate, but she loves to know that he will be carrying lovely memories to feed back into his thoughts.

While we're talking about language and things to say, it is well to touch also on what shouldn't be said. If I were you I would put away forever from my vocabulary such words as "frigid," "cold," or anything frosty that you might be tempted to hurl in a moment of letdown. As we have said, a woman has a way of becoming what you tell her she is. The language you use also has twenty-year ramifications.

Guard your words for propriety. Modesty is terribly important for some. Others react favorably to a sprinkling of "earthy" expressions. Some girls are terribly naïve. Others have heard too much. If I were you I would give some thought to the vocabulary of sex. You make a serious mistake whenever you build up defenses in her at any point, where you should be leaving thoughts of high expectation.

While we're on the praise and propriety theme be sure you make a swing by the store occasionally on your way home. How about some bewitching *odeur* or a gossamer wisp of something? A small remembrance like this now and then may be just the thing to back your words. You've got to save money someplace, but one place never to do it is on women's lingerie. Make your purchase and rhapsodize. Even with the high cost of beefsteak she'll love you for such extravagance.

Before I sign off let me remind you again what we've taught you at home as the basic fact about sex. This is that *sex is a gift of God and there is absolutely nothing negative about it when it's right.*

That, I'm sure you have discovered, is much easier to say than to practice. For more than twenty years the negative has been hurled at you from all points of the compass. All these things have left their imprint. Sometimes your imagination went wild and you wondered if you weren't one of the devil's angels with sex where your brains ought to be.

Then you met Marilyn and you *knew* that was good. But here, too, there was negative in the positive. You fought to control yourself and it was one grim battle for sure.

At last you were married! Great day! Suddenly it was legal! You were free to let yourself go. But there were still these old hangers-on, and how can a man view as all-good what he has been fighting as half-bad? The answer, of course, is that it will take time and patience and a gradual reorientation of your attitudes and hers.

So that's your aim. In my judgment it is one of the highest goals any husband can set for himself. To train yourself in the art of total manliness is a noble undertaking. To educate the woman you love in full expression of her womanliness, well, that's a privilege too great to describe in words.

I wish you the best. If you do give it your best, beginning right now, and stay with it carefully for something like twenty years, the time will come when you will know what the Bible means when it says, "male and female created he them ... and God saw everything that he had made, and, behold, it was very good."

Keep the home fires burning,

Dad

The Twenty-seventh Letter: Infidelity

Dear Phil,

It is late, but before I go to bed I want to tell you something I heard this evening. It follows hard on the heels of what I wrote you today about sex.

This man phoned while we were having dinner and he had to see me right then. So we met at our appointed spot and it was plain to see he was hurting.

He wasted no time getting to his problem. Before I could ask him the usual questions about family, business, or even "What's up?" he began pouring out his story.

Same song, next verse! Anyone who counsels with people hears it over and over and over—and you've already caught on. The poor devil *was* in serious trouble. His wife found out today that he is "playing around" (his words). When he arrived home this evening, there were his bags on the front step. She had packed them thoroughly and attached a note. His hand shook as he handed it to me. What it said was that she was through; tomorrow she would see a lawyer; she didn't care if she never laid eyes on him again; she would do all she could to fix it so he'd never see the children. She also said she hated him and, for all she cared, he could "drop dead!"

He was totally shattered. My heart went out to him. It always gets me to see a grown man cry and this was no exception. He admitted he had it coming. She had caught him in a carefully laid trap and was there anything I could do?

Time was when I thought the right thing at times like this was a sermon on the text "Be sure your sins will find you out." But that day is long gone. When a man confesses his guilt that freely, what he needs is an ear to hear him through; a hand to help him put the pieces back together; and a couple of feet headed in the direction of his house to see if she'll reconsider. She usually will if she is given some time to get her temperature down. When her rage subsides, the road looks terribly desolate as she sees herself going it alone with her children. Then, too, she begins to ask herself some questions about her place in their marriage and is she partly responsible?

So, I'll wait for a hunch that this is the hour and then I'll move in. You add your prayers to mine that we can get this nest back up there where it belongs.

But the things he kept saying that I wanted to pass on were these agonizing cries from deep inside: "How could I be such an ass? I don't blame her. I don't hate her. *But I sure do hate me!*"

In all my counseling with adulterers, it seems to me that this shame turned in on oneself is the major penalty. This is why the man who admits his guilt needs no lecturing from me. He'll give himself the full treatment, and it's pure hell for the fellow whose conscience is jumping up and down on his broken spirit. Of course if he won't admit it, that's something else. But even the refusal to come clean is often only a smoke screen to avoid facing the terrible truth.

This is how we are. When we were put together, our Creator wrote certain irrefutable laws in the heart of us men. One of these is that wrong must first be settled with Him before it can be made right elsewhere. No matter how we try to dodge it, the truth is that what we think of ourselves matters more in the long run than what other people think. This includes friends, enemies, em ployers, employees, neighbors, kinfolk, "the boys," "those guys," other women, and irate wives. We can go to the ends of the earth, or a million other places, to put distance between ourselves and anyone else. But because we are made as we are, we can never, ever, get away from us!

They say it is possible for a man to kill his conscience. But do you think he can? I've met a few who seemed to have that job done. Yet for each of these I've known dozens who had only pushed it so far down inside they simply couldn't hear it any more. Then one day it pushed over the tombstone where they thought they had buried it permanently. And from what I've seen there is nothing worse than these inner voices of integrity whispering, shouting, leering "Boo, remember me?"

This has to be one of the worst features of infidelity. No matter how much a man rationalizes his position, he knows he has taken a route that leads *away* from the real problem. He may be looking only for biological release. He may be getting sympathy from the other woman, which he doesn't feel from his wife. It may be that he is simply swept up in the excitement of clandestine amour. There may be numerous other satisfactions. But somehow they can never balance his failure to work things out right where he knows he should. He's failed at the one place where he wanted to succeed, and *this depreciates his opinion of himself.* He has taken the coward's way out, and men don't like cowards. At the heart of any male worthy of his name is the knowledge that great victories don't come cheap.

The further down life's road you go, the more you will learn that discipline, commitment, and plain, old-fashioned, manly guts are no small part of the thrill of living. The real prize comes only to the man who works things through until he can stand at the mirror and say, "Well, it wasn't easy! But I like what I see looking back at me."

It was foolish of me to overlook this part of the sex theme when I wrote you earlier today. The reason, you will realize, is a compliment to you. It never even crossed my mind that you would take the easy way. Knowing you as I do, I'm sure you'll work things out right where they should be worked out. But as I look back honestly on my own days of early marriage, I realize there were lots of things in my head that surprised and bothered me. Being a chip off the old block, the same thing may happen to you. It does to a lot of fellows. In fact, I've known plenty of men well enough to know that this is actually standard equipment on some of the best models.

When a man marries, he ties himself up to one woman because he has decided that she has what he wants, what he needs, what he longs for. Then, of all the crazy things—other women are still attractive. Maybe his sex life with his chosen isn't everything he thought it would be. Or, perhaps it is just great, thank you! Yet his mind continues to wander. There are still good-looking legs besides his wife's, and other feminine forms going by with devastating allure. Sometimes his thoughts are enough to make him wonder. Is he some kind of freak, maybe the number-one evil mind of all creation?

He isn't! Neither are you. You're a red-blooded, all-American, virile youth, and the more you're getting at home, the more thoughts of sex may be right up there at the fore in your head, your veins, your whole being!

So, what can you do about it? I mean after you accept it as natural and see it as a real challenge to your total manhood, what can you do?

One of the finest things you can do is to share your struggle with Marilyn. With me, inner battles shared with the person I love most are already half won. It was a great realization for me when I caught on to the fact that part of the perfect sex relationship is to be honest about everything, including the part that bamboozles a man and makes him feel like something out of the jungle.

Of course you must go at this right and pace the whole thing properly. But you can believe me, good women brought along carefully, have a wonderful facility for sharing these things. Even though they do not feel the sex urge like we feel it, they are equipped with something that enables them to understand male tendencies if we give them a chance. The woman who truly loves her man wants to know what he's thinking—all of it.

Your mother is a real ace at this, and I have a feeling Marilyn will be too if you do your part. One way to do it right is to develop your own honest versions of whatever it takes to get this message through: "All roads lead home! Thank you for being so great that all the interesting people I meet make me want to hurry back to where you are."

Then when you convince her that this is authentic, you can develop a nice little game between you. In it she says what she thinks and you do. She encourages you to talk freely about types you prefer, who you find interesting, what turns you on, and the whole bit. She has nothing to fear now. Neither do you. Your marriage is one of the rare ones where nobody hides, and, oh boy, how healthy!

Sex at its best is based on truth. At its best it is a spiritual relationship in which body, mind, and soul respond honestly with a song of praise to the Creator, who loves you so much that he made you to love each other.

This kind of sex is beautiful. It is holy. But it is also fun, and I hope for you that no small part of the fun will be developing things at home so you won't need to go elsewhere, because the real thing is right there, and nothing could be finer.

Faithfully,
Dad

P.S. One of the nicest things your mother ever did for me was shortly after we began sharing all these things. From somewhere she dug up this old proverb and wrote it on my heart:

> God doesn't keep the birds of temptation from flying over our heads. He only asks that we keep them from building nests in our hair!

Nice, isn't it? And it is so good to know that this is how it is.

The Twenty-eighth Letter: "Except the Lord Build the House"

Dear Phil,

One of the ancient Bible writers suggests that God is like a man with a lantern, going through time, looking for people on whom he can build his kingdom. Our hope for you and Marilyn is that he might one day say, "I've been looking for you a long time."

Even a quick glance down the road of history makes it plain that no civilization has qualified to date. Bleaching bones all over the place are solemn evidence that lots of people who thought they had it made didn't.

Do you suppose any race of men will ever get the job done? If so, how? One way we can be sure it won't come is like a lucky row of numbers on a bingo card. Strength of character doesn't develop by chance.

So where is our hope? Is it in churches more honest and up to date, finer schools, new forms of government? Will the kingdom come when our economy is finally balanced? Does it wait for an end of poverty, second-class citizenship, war? Or does it depend on greater technology, faster space craft, some fresh new influences from beyond our own planet?

Doubtless some combination of all these influences will be part of the eventual answer. But you can put me down as one who believes that *when life is finally what it ought to be, the major source of man's new greatness will be the home.* I'll put my money on this possibility—that the kingdom of God will come when the family is all it should be and marriage between the sons and daughters of the Lord has reached its full potential.

It does make sense, doesn't it? This is the place of our earliest influence. Over a normal life span most of us put in a major portion of our time at home. We experience our most intimate relationships there. From this base we learn most of our habits, develop most of our emotional reactions, make our first decisions on values. Small wonder poets tell us that this is life's number one shaper of destiny. It is.

What I hope I have given you here is the feeling that how well you succeed in your marriage may have an effect far down into eternity.

Yet a serious study of marriage these days does make us wonder. There are too many breaks in what ought to be solid, and cracks that shouldn't be.

Why does this happen? Nearly one hundred percent of those with whom I stand at the altar expect to live happily ever after. When they promise to cherish each other forever they really mean what they say. But one day the honeymoon ends and there are bills to pay and dishes to do and bosses to please and floors to scrub and more bills and more dishes and more bills and "Egad! Did you see this bill for insurance?" and she's talking about a new dishwasher and "Who spent $10.90 at the drugstore?" and "Why does he just sit there watching his stupid game, never making one move to help me with these dishes?"

So, this is the *real* ever after? What became of his sweet talk and where did her glamour go and "Why should I work so hard if he's not going to try?" and "This time it's her turn to apologize!"

Thus, little by little the foundation begins to weaken. Then one day she comes, or he comes, or they both come wanting to know what can be done to seal the rift and get things back like they were at the time of their lovely beginning.

Most ministers these days spend hours counseling with couples in some kind of trouble. You can take my word for it, those of us who deal with marital difficulties hear everything imaginable and some things you would hardly believe. To show you what I mean here are a few common and not-so-common quotes from my study-notebook:

"He won't talk." ... "She never shuts up." ... "His folks never come over." ... "Hers won't go away." ... "He drinks too much." ... "She overeats." ... "His manners are atrocious." ... "She thinks she's Lady Astor." ... "He thinks every move I make is a sex move." ... "The only thing she makes is excuses." ... "He needs a psychiatrist." ... "She's obviously off her rocker!"

I could go on like this for hours. Sometimes their problems are trivial. We wonder why they can't laugh. Others are rather simple. With adjustments here and there these breaks are easily mended. But then there are those in which matters have gone too far. There is little to do but weep now. These gaps are dreadfully wide and can anyone close this fissure?

Because this is how it is, I have come to believe that my part as third person at the altar is to say some things loud and clear before we get there. I am done marrying couples who want a big church wedding only because that's how they always dreamed it, or because some member of the family is sentimental, or because everybody who is anybody does it like this. From here on in I intend to say at the rehearsal:

"Except the Lord build the house they labor in vain who build it! Tomorrow this wedding begins with the words 'Dearly beloved we are assembled here in the presence of God to join this man and this woman in holy wedlock, which is instituted of God.' Don't ever forget it. This is no fashion show, nor a gathering of high society, nor a tip of tradition's hat before we adjourn for cocktails. We are coming together to establish a new home where the Lord can accomplish his purpose and establish his plan."

Of course there will be those who wonder "What's bugging him?" If anyone should voice the question, I could tell them what's bugging him. It is the steady parade of those who come with the broken pieces and broken vows and broken hearts.

Like I say, I really do think they meant it when they pledged their love "Till death do us part!" But here they are pointing the finger, blaming each other, excusing themselves, rationalizing, justifying the breakup—

"I simply don't care any more." ... "My feelings are thoroughly dead." ... "But you did care once, didn't you?" ... "You promised to love forever!" ... "O sure, that!" ... "But we were so immature!" ... "We didn't know all the involvements!" ... "I really don't think it could possibly work!"

They're right. It couldn't. It never could, ever, the way they've been building. The trouble is *no verticals!* Nothing but horizontals. No upward thrust.

This is why I spend considerable time in marriage consultation talking about prayer. In my opinion nothing, and I mean absolutely nothing, matters more than this: Can these two children of God accept the fact that he made them and brought them together to create something not first for themselves but first for him? And if they can believe this then the next question is: "Will you open the channels daily for his spirit to touch your spirits and his love to come into your home?"

I have seen marriages that looked for all the world like they were shattered beyond any earthly power to put them back together. And they were. But some of these are still going on and going greater than ever because they learned to pray. So help me, this is a fact. *I have never known one couple who prayed together who didn't find their marriage moving toward deeper understanding, growing inner joy, and a finer, fuller love.*

There will be days when you simply won't have time for all you would like to do. Almost everyone I know who has a living to earn and a home to manage feels harried and hurried more than he wishes he did. But the truth is that some people do manage to live with a kind of inner calm.

How do they do this? If you were to ask them they might tell you that they don't do it at all. The secret is that everything they do is done from an inner center of reference.

Your home can know this presence and set itself down in this peace. But it won't come without effort. This is why if I were you I would determine that nothing will take precedence over this—that you look to the Lord together at least once every day.

Sometimes it should be an unhurried block of time when you hold hands and discuss what you wish to pray about. Then you bow your heads and one of you prays aloud, or you both do, or maybe even better you pray silently, each talking to God as you understand him. Then there can be other days when you spend only a few moments for the vertical thrust.

The truth is that "How to pray?" isn't nearly as important as "Do you pray?" If you do pray, and pray regularly, you will be led to ways of prayer that are right for you and this is what matters.

So the rule for married prayers is: "We will pray for each other and with each other. Every day we will pray and the more we have to do the more we will remember to pray!"

Sure there are homes where God is left out and they never pray and still they hold together. I'm glad that's true. It is obvious that we need permanency of every kind. But from what I've seen this truth holds: *The kind of homes we most need are those where two lives are being drawn together by a holy love greater than their own.*

So we hope your tea leaves read well, and your crystal ball looks good, and the sign of your stars is promising. We wish you smooth sailing, calm waters, *bon voyage*. May fortune smile. May you have good luck.

All these we want for you and Marilyn plus every other happy hope the human mind could possibly concoct. But if, as so often is true, we would need to limit our wishes, then the one great wish we have for you is that you may learn to be open to Divine love.

Actually the truth is that God never quits loving. He's there one hundred percent of the time, knocking, waiting, hoping.

In the light of this truth, what any marriage needs is to keep in tune with the Infinite. When you do your part, he does his. And what he does is to draw your love to his in a sacred triune relationship.

Those who have experienced this can tell you there is no greater love.

Prayerfully,
Dad

The Twenty-ninth Letter: The Man Who Had a "Thing" About Guns

Dear Phil,

I used to hunt ducks with a man who had a "thing" about his guns. He also had a "thing" about my gun. He polished his with some special kind of oil, which smelled like bananas. And he ate me out in the blind whenever the ducks weren't flying because my gun didn't smell like bananas. In fact, my gun even had some scratches on the brown part. It also had some terrible stuff called "pitting" in the barrel and he said this was because I didn't clean it first thing when I got home after a hunt.

But there were some good reasons why I kept hunting with this firearm perfectionist. He was a member of the best duck lease on the river and I wasn't. He was also chairman of the board at our church and we could talk business to and fro. The third reason wasn't so good. He was having trouble with his wife and I hoped we might be able to save the marriage.

But we couldn't. Finally, she gave up. They got a divorce. It was one of those cases that would make a grown man cry. There he would sit in his beautiful den—antelope heads, stuffed pheasants, lush white rug made from the hide of a mountain goat, cabinet full of beautiful guns all polished with oil that smelled like bananas.

He would stand there by the case taking them out and handling them with tender, loving care. Then he would remember the way my gun looked and take off again on one of his diatribes about the care of guns. This never failed to shame me and I would go home determined to get out my gun and clean it like it had never been cleaned before.

But do you know what happened? When I arrived home, she would be waiting for me at the door. So we would sit down on our rocking love seat, hold hands, visit, and like that. In less time than it takes to look into her eyes, I completely forgot my noble resolve to love my gun with more devotion.

The other day as I was thinking back on all this, a great idea occurred to me. Funny, isn't it, how we so often get these brilliant thoughts too late?

What happened was that my banana-oil brother would *always* include in his lectures at least one reference like this: "I just can't understand how a man could invest so much in a gun and then let it go to pot!"

The thought that came to me was, "Why didn't I figure up how much it cost him to get his wife? Courtship expenses—movies, flowers, dinners, gifts, postage, the wedding. All the food she's eaten through the years, clothes she's bought, medicine. It really would be a tidy sum, wouldn't it?"

Then I could have said, "My dear Whoozit! You are absolutely right! Let us now turn your brilliant observation to other things. Isn't a man a fool to invest so much in marriage and then let it go to pot?"

He sure would be, wouldn't he?

Carry on,
Dad